Russian Phrases FOR DUMMIES

by Andrew Kaufman, PhD,
and Serafima Gettys, PhD,
with Nina Wieda

1807
WILEY
2007

Wiley Publishing, Inc.

Russian Phrases For Dummies®

Published by
Wiley Publishing, Inc.
111 River St
Hoboken, NJ 07030-5774
www.wiley.com

Copyright © 2007 by Wiley Publishing, Inc., Indianapolis, Indiana

Published by Wiley Publishing, Inc., Indianapolis, Indiana

Published simultaneously in Canada

For general information on our other products and services, please contact our Customer Care Department within the U.S. at 800-762-2974, outside the U.S. at 317-572-3993, or fax 317-572-4002.

For technical support, please visit www.wiley.com/techsupport.

Wiley also publishes its books in a variety of electronic formats. Some content that appears in print may not be available in electronic books.

Library of Congress Control Number: 2007932467

ISBN: 978-0-470-14974-4

Manufactured in the United States of America

10 9 8 7 6 5 4 3 2

About the Authors

Andrew Kaufman, PhD, is currently a Visiting Lecturer in the Department of Slavic Languages and Literatures at the University of Virginia. He holds a PhD in Slavic Languages and Literatures from Stanford University, and he has recognized success as both a published scholar and an innovative, award-winning teacher of Russian language, literature, and culture at some of the country's top universities. To learn more about Dr. Kaufman, please visit his website at www.professorandy.com.

Serafima Gettys, PhD, earned her doctorate degree in Foreign Language Education from Gertzen State Pedagogical University, Leningrad, USSR. She is currently a Coordinator of the Foreign Language Program at Lewis University, where she also teaches Russian. Prior to coming to Lewis University, she taught Russian at Stanford University. Gettys is also a member of a number of professional language associations.

Nina Wieda is a doctoral student in Slavic Languages and Literatures at Northwestern University in Chicago. A trained linguist with an MA in Social Sciences, Nina also has a book of poetry published in Russian, and a number of scholarly articles on Chekhov and contemporary drama published in English.

Publisher's Acknowledgments

We're proud of this book; please send us your comments through our Dummies online registration form located at www.dummies.com/register/.

Some of the people who helped bring this book to market include the following:

Acquisitions, Editorial, and Media Development

Compiler: Laura Peterson-Nussbaum

Project Editor: Elizabeth Kuball

Acquisitions Editor: Tracy Boggier

Copy Editor: Elizabeth Kuball

Technical Editor: Maria Kuruskina

Editorial Manager: Michelle Hacker

Editorial Supervisor and Reprint Editor: Carmen Krikorian

Editorial Assistant: Erin Calligan Mooney, Joe Niesen, Leeann Harney, David Lutton

Cartoons: Rich Tennant, www.the5thwave.com

Composition

Project Coordinator: Heather Kolter

Layout and Graphics: Stephanie D. Jumper, Heather Ryan, Julie Trippetti, Christine Williams, Erin Zeltner

Anniversary Logo Design: Richard Pacifico

Proofreaders: Jacqui Brownstein, Charles Spencer

Indexer: Broccoli Information Management

Publishing and Editorial for Consumer Dummies

Diane Graves Steele, Vice President and Publisher, Consumer Dummies

Joyce Pepple, Acquisitions Director, Consumer Dummies

Kristin A. Cocks, Product Development Director, Consumer Dummies

Michael Spring, Vice President and Publisher, Travel

Kelly Regan, Editorial Director, Travel

Publishing for Technology Dummies

Andy Cummings, Vice President and Publisher, Dummies Technology/General User

Composition Services

Gerry Fahey, Vice President of Production Services

Debbie Stailey, Director of Composition Services

Table of Contents

Chapter 13: Ten Phrases That Make
You Sound Russian 189

The 5th Wave

By Rich Tennant

"Honey, please! Be patient! How's anyone going to know what's wrong unless I find the Russian word for 'alligator'?"

Introduction

● ●

*S*peaking more than one language is like living more than one life, one of the ancient philosophers said. And it's true — traveling in a foreign country such as Russia suddenly becomes a lot more exciting when you can engage in elegant small talk with a hotel receptionist, compliment your tour guide's dress, or actually read the menu and order the food that you really want. Being able to ask for things instead of pointing at them, and being able to get directions from the locals instead of staring at a map, are some of the little things that make you feel at home.

You don't even need to cross the ocean to immerse yourself in Russian culture; you can find little Russian neighborhoods (or even pretty big ones!) in many American cities. Whether your colleagues, your neighbors, or your friends speak Russian, the best way to win their hearts is to speak their language to them.

Now, *Russian Phrases For Dummies* won't make you a fluent reader of Dostoevsky in the original (most Russians themselves need somewhat of a preparation for that). It will, however, equip you with phrases necessary to function in many real-life situations, from shopping to visiting the theater. So, buckle up, and good luck on your journey! Or, as the Russians like to say, **Zhelayem vam udachi!** (zhih-*lah*-eem vahm oo-*dah*-chee; We wish you good luck!)

About This Book

The best thing about *Russian Phrases For Dummies* is that you don't have to read all the way through it to get the information you need. You can open the table of contents, find the section that interests you at the moment, and start talking! You don't have to read the previous chapters to understand any of the sections of this book

Another thing you don't need to do is memorize long vocabulary lists or grammar rules. We give you ready-made phrases; you just need to read them and start using them right away to impress your Russian friends!

Conventions Used in This Book

Here are some conventions that allow you to navigate through this book with maximum ease:

- ✔ We present Russian phrases in transliteration (Russian sounds represented with English characters). You can see the Cyrillic alphabet in Chapter 1. Russian terms are easily found in the text because they're set in **boldface**.

- ✔ Each Russian word is followed by its pronunciation and English translation in parentheses. In each pronunciation, the stressed syllable is in *italics*.

A little example to give you an idea of what we mean: The phrase for "I love you" in Russian is **Ya tebya lyublyu.** (ya tee-*b'ah* l'oo-*bl'oo;* I love you).

Foolish Assumptions

When we started writing this book, we tried to imagine what our future reader was going to be like. In the end, we came up with a list of foolish assumptions about who we think wants to read this book. Do you recognize yourself in these descriptions?

- ✔ You know no Russian — or if you took Russian in high school or college, you don't remember a word of it.

✔ You're not looking for a book that will make you
  fluent in Russian; you just want to know some
  words, phrases, and content constructions so
  that you can communicate basic information in
  Russian.

✔ You don't want to have to memorize long lists of
  vocabulary words or a bunch of boring grammar rules.

✔ You want to have fun and learn a little bit of
  Russian at the same time.

Icons Used in This Book

For your convenience, we marked some information
in this book with special icons. Check out this guide
to the icons, and the next time you see one of them,
you'll know what to expect!

From famous Russian writers to a polite way
to decline an invitation, this icon marks a
wide variety of curious and useful facts
about Russian culture.

If you're curious about how the Russian language works, and if you want to expand your
command of Russian to the extent of making
up your own phrases, these bits of grammatical information may be of interest to you.

This icon points out some important
information about Russian that's worth
remembering.

This icon signals a useful bit of information
that can make life easier for you, whether it's
a handy way to remember a useful word or
an insider's advice on how to better handle a
certain situation.

This icon draws your attention to something
you need to know to avoid a common mistake.

Where to Go from Here

Go ahead and start anywhere. You don't have to read in a specific order. Just choose a topic that seems appealing, find the corresponding chapter in the table of contents, and start speaking Russian!

If you've never taken Russian before, you may want to read Chapters 1 and 2 before tackling the later chapters. They give you some basics, such as how to pronounce the sounds.

Chapter 1

I Say It How? Speaking Russian

In This Chapter
▶ Understanding the Russian alphabet
▶ Pronouncing words properly
▶ Discovering popular expressions

*W*elcome to Russian! Whether you want to read a Russian menu, enjoy Russian music, or just chat it up with your Russian friends, this is the beginning of your journey. In this chapter, you get all the letters of the Russian alphabet, discover the basic rules of Russian pronunciation, and say some popular Russian expressions and idioms.

Looking at the Russian Alphabet

If you're like most English speakers, you probably think that the Russian alphabet is the most challenging aspect of picking up the language. But not to worry. The Russian alphabet isn't as hard as you think.

From A to Ya: Making sense of Cyrillic

The Russian alphabet is based on the Cyrillic alphabet, which was named after the ninth-century Byzantine monk, Cyril. But throughout this book, we convert all the letters into familiar Latin symbols, which are the same symbols we use in the English alphabet. This process of converting from Cyrillic to Latin letters is known as *transliteration*. We list the Cyrillic alphabet here in case you're adventurous and brave enough to prefer reading real Russian instead of being fed with the ready-to-digest Latin version of it. And even if you don't want to read the real Russian, check out Table 1-1 to find out what the whole fuss is about regarding the notorious "Russian alphabet."

Notice that, in most cases, a transliterated letter corresponds to the way it's actually pronounced. As a rule, you may assume that the transliteration fairly well represents the actual pronunciation. The biggest exceptions to this are the letter **Йй,** which is transcribed as **j** but pronounced like an English *y,* and the soft sign **Ьь,** which is transcribed as ' but only softens the preceding consonant.

Scholars do not agree on the letter **j.** Some believe that it's a consonant; others think that it's a vowel. We don't want to take sides in this matter and are listing it both as a consonant and a vowel.

Consonants are pronounced softly if they a re followed by **ye, yo, ya,** or **yu** (**е, ё, я, ю**). These letters (**ye, yo, ya,** and **yu**) preserve the *y* sound if they are at the beginning of the word (as in *yes, your, yard,* and *youth*).

Table 1-1	The Russian Alphabet in Cyrillic		
The Letter in Cyrillic	**Transliteration (The Corresponding Letter or Sound in the English Alphabet)**	**Pronunciation**	**Vowel or Consonant**
Aa	A	*ah* if stressed as in f<u>a</u>ther; *uh* if appearing in any unstressed syllable, as in hum<u>a</u>n	Vowel

The Letter in Cyrillic	Transliteration (The Corresponding Letter or Sound in the English Alphabet)	Pronunciation	Vowel or Consonant
Бб	B	*b* as in <u>b</u>ook; *p* if at the end of the word	Consonant
Вв	V	*v* as in <u>v</u>ictor; *f* if at the end of the word	Consonant
Гг	G	*g* as in <u>g</u>reat; *k* if at the end of the word	Consonant
Дд	D	*d* as in <u>d</u>uck; *t* if at the end of the word	Consonant
Ее	Ye	*ye* as in <u>ye</u>s if at the beginning of the word; *eh* as in t<u>e</u>n if preceded by any consonant, making that consonant sound soft; *ee* as in s<u>ee</u>k if appearing in any unstressed syllable before a stressed syllable; *eh* after a stressed syllable and at the end of the word, making the preceding consonant sound softly	Vowel
Ёё	Yo	*yo* as in <u>yo</u>ur	Vowel
Жж	Zh	*zh* as mea<u>s</u>ure; *sh* if at the end of the word	Consonant
Зз	Z	*z* as in <u>z</u>ebra; *s* if at the end of the word	Consonant
Ии	I	*ee* as in p<u>ee</u>k	Vowel

(continued)

Table 1-1 *(continued)*

The Letter in Cyrillic	Transliteration (The Corresponding Letter or Sound in the English Alphabet)	Pronunciation	Vowel or Consonant
Йй	J	very short *y* as boy or May	Vowel or Consonant
Кк	K	*k* as in <u>k</u>ing	Consonant
Лл	L	*l* as in <u>l</u>amp	Consonant
Мм	M	*m* as in <u>m</u>ommy	Consonant
Нн	N	*n* as in <u>n</u>ote	Consonant
Оо	O	*oh* as in as in t<u>a</u>lk; *ah* as in p<u>a</u>rk, if appearing one syllable before the stressed syllable; *uh* as in Morm<u>o</u>n, if appearing in any other unstressed syllable	Vowel
Пп	P	*p* as in <u>p</u>ort	Consonant
Рр	R	flap *r,* similar to trilled *r* in Spanish, as in mad<u>r</u>e, for example	Consonant
Сс	S	*s* as in <u>s</u>ort	Consonant
Тт	T	*t* as in <u>t</u>ie	Consonant
Уу	U	*oo* as sh<u>oo</u>t	Vowel
Фф	F	*f* as in <u>f</u>act	Consonant
Хх	Kh	*kh* like you're clearing your throat, or like the German *ch*	Consonant

The Letter in Cyrillic	Transliteration (The Corresponding Letter or Sound in the English Alphabet)	Pronunciation	Vowel or Consonant
Цц	Ts	*ts* as in ca<u>ts</u>	Consonant
Чч	Ch	*ch* as in <u>ch</u>air	Consonant
Шш	Sh	*sh* as in <u>sh</u>ock	Consonant
Щщ	Sh'	soft *sh*, as in <u>sh</u>eep	Consonant
ъ	"	hard sign (makes the preceding letter hard)	Neither
Ыы	Y	*Ih* (similar to *i* in bi<u>g</u>)	Vowel
ь	'	soft sign (makes the preceding letter soft)	Neither
Ээ	E	*e* as in <u>e</u>nd	Vowel
Юю	Yu	*yu* as in <u>u</u>se if at the beginning of the word; *oo* as in t<u>oo</u>th if preceded by any consonant, making that consonant sound soft	Vowel
Яя	Ya	*ya* if stressed as in <u>ya</u>rd; if at the beginning of the word; *ah* if preceded by any consonant, making that consonant sound soft; *ee* if unstressed and not in the final syllable of the word; *uh* if unstressed and in the final syllable of the word	Vowel

I know you! Familiar-looking, same-sounding letters

You may notice that some of the Russian letters in the previous section look a lot like English letters. The letters that look like English and are pronounced like English letters are

- ✔ Аа
- ✔ Кк
- ✔ Мм
- ✔ Оо
- ✔ Тт

Whenever you read Russian text, you should be able to recognize and pronounce these letters right away.

Playing tricks: Familiar-looking, different-sounding letters

Some Russian letters look like English letters but are pronounced differently. You want to watch out for these:

- ✔ **Вв:** It looks like English Bb, at least the capital letter does, but it's pronounced like the sound *v* as in *victor* or *vase.*

- ✔ **Ее:** This one's a constant annoyance for English speakers, who want to pronounce it like *ee,* as in the English word *geese.* In Russian, it's pronounced that way only if it appears in an unstressed syllable. Otherwise, if it appears in a stressed syllable, it is pronounced like *ye* as in *yes.*

- ✔ **Ёё:** Don't confuse this with the letter **Ее.** When two dots appear over the Ee, it's considered a different letter, and it's pronounced like *yo* as in *your.*

- ✔ **Нн:** It's not the English Hh — it just looks like it. Actually, it's pronounced like *n* as in *nick.*

- ✔ **Рр:** In Russian it's pronounced like a trilled *r* and not like the English letter *p* as in *pick*.

- ✔ **Сс:** This letter is always pronounced like *s* as in *sun* and never like *k* as in *victor*.

- ✔ **Уу:** This letter is pronounced like *oo* as in *shoot* and never like *y* as in *yes*.

- ✔ **Хх:** Never pronounce this letter like *z* or *ks* as in the word *Xerox*. In Russian, the sound it represents is a coarse-sounding, guttural *kh*, similar to the German *ch*. (See "Surveying sticky sounds," later in this chapter, for info on pronouncing this sound.)

How bizarre: Weird-looking letters

As you've probably noticed, quite a few Russian letters don't look like English letters at all:

- ✔ Бб
- ✔ Гг
- ✔ Дд
- ✔ Жж
- ✔ Зз
- ✔ Ии
- ✔ Йй
- ✔ Лл
- ✔ Пп
- ✔ Фф
- ✔ Цц
- ✔ Чч
- ✔ Шш
- ✔ Щщ
- ✔ ъ
- ✔ Ыы
- ✔ ь
- ✔ Ээ
- ✔ Юю
- ✔ Яя

Don't panic over these letters. Just because they look weird doesn't mean they're any harder to say than the others. It's just a matter of memorizing their proper pronunciations. (Refer to Table 1-1 for details on how to say each letter.)

You may recognize several of these weird letters, such as **Ф, Г, Э, Л, П,** from learning the Greek alphabet during your fraternity or sorority days.

Sounding Like a Real Russian with Proper Pronunciation

Compared to English pronunciation, which often has more exceptions than rules, Russian rules of pronunciation are fairly clear and consistent.

Understanding the one-letter/ one-sound principle

Russian is a *phonetic language,* which means that for the most part one Russian letter corresponds to one sound. For example, the letter **K** is always pronounced like *k,* and the letter **M** is always pronounced like *m.*

Giving voice to vowels

Vowels are the musical building blocks of every Russian word. If you flub a consonant or two, you'll probably still be understood. But if you don't pronounce your vowels correctly, there's a good chance you won't be understood at all. So it's a good idea to get down the basic principles of saying Russian vowels.

That's stretching it: Lengthening out vowels

If you want to sound more Russian, don't shorten your vowels like English speakers often do. When you say **a, o,** open your mouth wider and purposefully stretch out the sounds to make them a little bit longer. Imagine, for example, that you're in your room on the second floor, and your mom is downstairs in the kitchen. You call her by saying "Mo-o-o-m!" That's the way Russians say their vowels (except for the shouting part!).

Some stress is good: Accenting the right vowels

Stress is an important concept in Russian. Putting a stress in the wrong place isn't just a formal mistake. It can hinder communication, because the meaning of a word can change based on where the stress is. For example, the word **zamok** (*zah*-muhk) means "castle." However, if you shift the stress from the first syllable to the last, the word **zamok** (zuh-*mohk*) now means "lock."

Unfortunately, no hard-and-fast rules about stress exist. Before learning a new Russian word, find out which vowel to stress. Look in any Russian-English dictionary, which usually marks stress by putting the sign ´ over the stressed syllable. In a dictionary, **zamok** (*zah*-muhk; castle) is written за'мок, and zamok (zuh-mohk; lock) is written замо'к.

Vowels misbehavin': Reduction

Some Russian letters change their behavior depending on whether they're in a stressed or an unstressed syllable. The vowels **a, o, ye,** and **ya** do this a lot. When stressed, they behave normally and are pronounced in the usual way, but when they're in an unstressed position, they go through a process called *reduction*. This deviation in the vowels' behavior is a very important linguistic phenomenon that deserves your special attention:

- **O,** which is normally pronounced like *oh,* sounds like *ah* (like the letter **a** in the word father) if it occurs exactly one syllable before the stressed syllable, and like a neutral *uh* (like the letter **a** in the word *about*) if it appears in any other unstressed syllable.

- **A,** which is pronounced like *ah* when it's stressed, is pronounced like a neutral *uh* (like the letter **a** in the word *about*) if it appears in any unstressed syllable.

The honest-to-goodness truth is that when the letter **a** appears in the syllable preceding the stressed syllable, its pronunciation is somewhere between *uh* and *ah*. We don't, however, want to burden you with excessive linguistic information, so we indicate the letter **a** as *uh* in all unstressed positions. Moreover, in conversational speech, catching the distinction is nearly impossible. If you say an unstressed **a** as *uh*, people will fully understand you.

✔ **Ye,** which is pronounced like *ye* (as in *yet*) in a stressed syllable, sounds like *ee* (as in *seek*) in any unstressed syllable.

When it appears at the end of a word, as in **viditye** (*vee*-dee-tee; [you] see [plural and formal singular]), or after another vowel, as in **chayepitiye** (chee-ee-*pee*-tee-eh; tea drinking), unstressed **ye** sounds like *eh* after another vowel at the end of the word.

✔ An unstressed **ya** sounds either like *ee* (as in *peek*) if it's unstressed (but not in the word's final syllable) or like *yuh* if it's unstressed in the final syllable of the word and also preceded by another vowel or **ь;** if it is preceded by a consonant, it is pronounced as *uh* and the preceding consonant is pronounced softly.

Here are some examples of how vowel reduction affects word pronunciation:

✔ You write **Kolorado** (Colorado) but say kuh-lah-*rah*-duh. Notice how the first **o** is reduced to a neutral *uh* and the next **o** is reduced to an *ah* sound (because it's exactly one syllable before the stressed syllable), and it's reduced again to a neutral *uh* sound in the final unstressed syllable.

✔ You write **khorosho** (good, well) but say khuh-rah-*shoh*. Notice how the first **o** is reduced to a neutral *uh*, the next **o** is reduced to *ah* (it precedes the stressed syllable), and **o** in the last syllable is pronounced as *oh* because it's stressed.

✔ You write **napravo** (to the right) but say nuh-*prah*-vuh. Notice that the first **a** is reduced to a neutral *uh* (because it's not in the stressed syllable), the second **a** is pronounced normally (like *ah*) and the final **o** is pronounced like a neutral *uh,* because it follows the stressed syllable.

✔ You write **Pyetyerburg** (Petersburg) but say pee-teer-*boork*. Notice how **ye** is reduced to the sound *ee* in each case, because it's not stressed.

✔ You write **Yaponiya** (Japan) but say yee-*poh*-nee-uh. Notice how the unstressed letter **ya** sounds like *yee* at the beginning of the word and like *ye* at the end of the word (because it's unstressed and in the final syllable).

Saying sibilants with vowels

The letters **zh, ts, ch, sh,** and **sh'** are called *sibilants,* because they emit a hissing sound. When certain vowels appear after these letters, those vowels are pronounced slightly differently than normal. After a sibilant, **ye** is pronounced like *eh* (as in *end*) and **yo** is pronounced like *oh* (as in *talk*). Examples are the words **tsyentr** (tsehntr; center) and **shyol** (shohl; went by foot [masculine]). The sound *ee* always becomes *ih* after one of these sibilants, regardless of whether the *ee* sound comes from the letter **i** or from an unstressed **ye** before the stressed syllable. Take, for example, the words **mashina** (muh-*shih*-nuh; car) and **shyestoy** (shih-*stohy*; the sixth).

Enunciating consonants correctly

Like Russian vowels, Russian consonants follow certain patterns and rules of pronunciation. If you want to sound like a real Russian, you need to keep the basics in the following sections in mind.

Say it, don't spray it! Relaxing with consonants

When pronouncing the letters **p, t,** or **k,** English speakers are used to straining their tongue and lips. This strain results in what linguists call *aspiration* — a burst of air that comes out of your mouth as you say these sounds. To see what we're talking about, put your hand in front of your mouth and say the word *top*. You should feel air against your hand as you pro nounce the word.

In Russian, however, aspiration shouldn't happen because consonants are pronounced without aspiration. In fact, you should totally relax your tongue and lips before saying Russian **p, t,** or **k.** To practice saying consonants without unnecessary aspiration, again put your hand in front of your mouth and say Russian cognates **park** (pahrk), **lampa** (*lahm-puh*), and **tank** (tahnk). Practice until you don't produce a puff of air with these words!

Cat got your tongue? Consonants losing their voice

Some consonants (**b, v, g, d, zh,** and **z**) are called *voiced consonants* because they're pronounced with the voice. But when voiced consonants appear at the end of a word, they actually lose their voice. This process is called *devoicing.* They're still spelled the same, but in their pronunciation, they transform into their devoiced counterparts:

- ✔ **B** is pronounced like *p.*
- ✔ **V** is pronounced like *f.*
- ✔ **G** is pronounced like *k.*
- ✔ **D** is pronounced like *t.*
- ✔ **Zh** is pronounced like *sh.*
- ✔ **Z** is pronounced like *s.*

Here are some examples:

- ✔ You write **Smirnov** but pronounce it as smeer-*nohf* because **v** at the end of the word is pronounced like *f.*
- ✔ You write **garazh** (garage) but say guh-*rahsh,* because at the end of the word, **zh** loses its voice and is pronounced like *sh.*

Nutty clusters: Pronouncing consonant combinations

Russian speech often sounds like an endless flow of consonant clusters. Combinations of two, three, and even four consonants are quite common. Take, for example, the common word for *hello* in Russian — **zdravstvujtye** (*zdrah*-stvooy-teh), which has two difficult consonant combinations (**zdr** and **stv**). Or take the word for *opinion* in Russian — **vzglyad** (vzglyat). The word contains four consonants following one another: **vzgl**.

How in the world do Russians say these words without choking? They practice, and so should you. Here are some words that contain consonant clusters you may want to repeat at leisure:

- **obstoyatyel'stvo** (uhp-stah-*ya*-tehl'-stvuh; circumstance)

- **pozdravlyat'** (puh-zdruhv-*lyat';* to congratulate)

- **prestuplyeniye** (pree-stoo-*plyen*-ee-ye; crime)

- **Rozhdyestvo** (ruzh-deest-*voh;* Christmas)

- **vzdor** (vzdohr; nonsense)

- **vzglyanut'** (vzglee-*noot';* to look/glance)

Surveying sticky sounds

Some Russian letters and sounds are hard for speakers of English. Take a look at some of them and find out how to pronounce them.

The bug sound zh

This sound corresponds to the letter Жж. It looks kind of like a bug, doesn't it? It sounds like a bug, too! In pronouncing it, try to imitate the noise produced by a bug flying over your ear — *zh-zh-zh* . . . The sound is similar to the sound in the words *pleasure* or *measure.*

The very short i sound

This sound corresponds to the letter **Йй**. This letter's name is *i kratkoye*, which literally means "a very short i," but it actually sounds like the very short English *y*. This sound is what you hear when you say the word *boy*. You should notice your tongue touching the roof of your mouth when you say this sound.

The rolled sound r

This sound corresponds to the letter **Рр** in the Russian alphabet. To say it correctly, begin by saying an English *r* and notice that your tongue is rolled back. Now begin moving your tongue back, closer to your upper teeth and try to say this sound with your tongue in this new position. You'll hear how the quality of the sound changes. This is the way the Russians say it.

The guttural sound kh

The corresponding Russian letter is **Хх**. To say it, imagine that you're eating and a piece of food just got stuck in your throat. What's the first reflex your body responds with? Correct! You will try to cough it up. Remember the sound your throat produces? This is the Russian sound *kh*. It's similar to the German *ch*.

The revolting sound y

To say this sound correctly, imagine that you're watching something really revolting, like an episode or *Survivor,* where the participants are gorging on a plate of swarming bugs. Now recall the sound you make in response to this. This sound is pronounced something like *ih,* and that's how you pronounce the Russian **ы** (the transliteration is *y*). Because this letter appears in some of the most commonly used words, including **ty** (tih; you [informal]), **vy** (vih; you [formal singular and plural]), and **my** (mih; we), it's important to say it as best you can.

The hard sign

This is the letter **Ъ**. Although the soft sign makes the preceding sound soft (see the next section), the hard sign makes it — yes, you guessed it — hard. The good news is that this letter (which transliterates to ") is rarely ever used in contemporary Russian. And even when it is, it doesn't change the pronunciation of the word. So, why does Russian have this sign? For two purposes:

✔ To harden the previous consonant

✔ To retain the hardness of the consonant before the vowels **ye, yo, yu,** and **ya,** which must be pronounced like at the beginning of the word.

Without the hard sign, these consonants would normally *palatalize* (soften). When a hard sign ъ separates a consonant and one of these vowels, the consonant is pronounced without palatalization, as in the word **pod"yezd** (pahd-*yezd;* porch), for example. However, don't worry too much about this one if your native language is English. Native speakers of English rarely tend to palatalize their Russian consonants the way Russians do it. In other words, if you're a native English speaker and you come across the situation described here, you probably make your consonant hard and, therefore, pronounce it correctly by default!

The soft sign

This is the letter ь (transliterated to '), and it doesn't have a sound. Its only mission in life is to make the preceding consonant soft. This sound is very important in Russian because it can change the meaning of a word. For example, without the soft sign, the word **mat'** (maht'; mother) becomes **mat,** which means "obscene language." And when you add a soft sign at the end of the word **von** (vohn; over there), it becomes **von'** (vohn') and means "stench." See how important the soft sign is?

It is also used retain the softness of the consonant before the vowels **ye, yo, yu,** and **ya,** which must be pronounced as at the beginning of the word — for example, **v'yuga** (*v'yoo*-guh; blizzard). Another very important function of ь is that it shows the grammatical gender (feminine) if it follows a sibilant at the end of the word; in this case, **ь** does not affect pronunciation. Compare **myech** (mehch; sword [masculine]) and **noch'** (nohch; night [feminine]).

So, here's how you can make consonants soft:

1. **Say the consonant — for example,** l, t, **or** d.

   Note where your tongue is. What you should feel is that the tip of your tongue is touching the ridge of your upper teeth and the rest of the tongue is hanging in the mouth like a hammock in the garden on a nice summer day.

2. **While you're still pronouncing the consonant, raise the body of your tongue and press it against the hard palate.**

   Can you hear how the quality of the consonant has changed? It sounds much softer now, doesn't it? That's how you make your consonants soft.

Chapter 2

Grammar on a Diet: Just the Basics

*O*ne of the biggest differences between English and Russian is that English tends to have a fixed order of words, whereas Russian enjoys a free order of words.

In English, word order can often determine the meaning of a sentence. For example, in English you say, "The doctor operated on the patient," but you never say, "The patient operated on the doctor." It just doesn't make sense.

In Russian, you can freely shift around the order of words in a sentence, because the Russian case system tells you exactly what role each word plays in the sentence. What's a case? Read on.

Making the Russian Cases

In a Russian sentence, every noun, pronoun, and adjective takes a different ending depending on the case it's in. Cases are sets of endings that words take to indicate their function and relationship to other words in the sentence. Russian has 6 cases, which isn't that bad compared to Finnish, which has 15.

Nominative case

A noun (or a pronoun or an adjective) always appears in the nominative case in an English-Russian dictionary. Its main function is to indicate the subject of the sentence. For example, in the sentence **Bryenda izuchayet russkij yazyk** (*brehn*-duh ee-zoo-*chah*-eht *roos*-keey yee-*zihk;* Brenda studies Russian), the word Bryenda, is the subject of the sentence and consequently is used in the nominative case.

Genitive case

Use the genitive case to indicate possession. It answers the question "Whose?" In the phrase **kniga Anny** (*knee*-guh *ah*-nih; Anna's book), **Anna** is in the genitive case **(Anny)** because she's the book's owner.

Accusative case

The accusative case mainly indicates a direct object, which is the object of the action of the verb in a sentence. For example, in the sentence **Ya lyublyu russkij yazyk** (yah l'oou-*bl'oo roo*-skeey yee-*zihk;* I love Russian), the phrase **russkij yazyk** is in the accusative case because it's the direct object.

Dative case

Use the dative case to indicate an indirect object, which is the person or thing toward whom the action in a sentence is directed. For example, in the sentence **Ya dal uchityelyu sochinyeniye** (yah dahl oo-*chee*-tee-lyu suh-chee-*n'eh*-nee-eh; I gave the teacher my essay), **uchityelyu** (oo-*chee*-tee-lyu; teacher) is in the dative case because it's the indirect object.

Use the dative case after certain prepositions such as **k** (k; toward) and **po** (poh; along).

Instrumental case

As the name suggests, the instrumental case is often used to indicate the instrument that assists in the carrying out of an action. So, when you say that you're writing a letter with a **ruchka** (*rooch*-kuh; pen), you have to put **ruchka** into the instrumental case, which is **ruchkoj** (*rooch*-kuhy).

Use the instrumental case after certain prepositions such as **s** (s; with), **myezhdu** (*m'ehzh*-doo; between), **nad** (naht; over), **pod** (poht; below), and **pyeryed** (*p'eh*-reet; in front of).

Prepositional case

Only used after certain prepositions. Older Russian textbooks often refer to it as the *locative case,* because it often indicates the location where the action takes place. It's used with the prepositions **v** (v; in), **na** (nah; on), **o** (oh; about), and **ob** (ohb; about).

By the way, you may wonder why the English preposition "about" is translated by two different Russian equivalents: **o** and **ob.** For your information, **o** is used if the following word begins with a consonant. Use **ob** if the following word begins with a vowel.

Building Your Grammar Base with Nouns and Pronouns

Nouns and pronouns are the building blocks of any sentence. In the following sections, you find out about genders, cases, and plurals of nouns.

Getting the lowdown on the gender of nouns

Unlike English nouns, every Russian noun has what's called a *grammatical gender:* masculine, feminine, or neuter. Knowing a noun's gender is important because it determines how the noun changes for each of the six cases.

The ending of a noun in its dictionary form (the nominative case) indicates the noun's gender in most cases. Nouns ending in a consonant and **j** (an unusual letter) are masculine. Nouns ending in **a** or **ya** are feminine. If nouns end in **o, ye,** or **yo,** they are neuter. Nouns can be either feminine or masculine if they end in the soft sign (**'**).

Grammatical gender for words denoting living beings, in the majority of cases, coincides with biological gender. The word **mal'chik** (*mahl'*-cheek; boy) is a masculine noun and the word **dyevushka** (*d'eh*-voosh-kuh; girl) is a feminine noun, just as you'd expect.

Checking out cases for nouns

Noun declension is when you change the case endings for nouns. Table 2-1 shows you the declension for masculine, feminine, and neuter singular nouns for all the cases.

Table 2-1			Declension of Singular Nouns			
If a Noun in Its Dictionary Form (Nominative Case) Ends In	To Form Genitive	To Form Accusative	To Form Dative	To Form Instrumental	To Form Prepositional
A consonant	Add **a**.	Add **a** if the noun is a living being; otherwise, don't do anything.	Add **u**.	Add **om**.	Add **ye**.
a	Replace **a** with **y**.	Replace **a** with **u**.	Replace **a** with **ye**.	Replace **a** with **oj**.	Replace **a** with **ye**.
iye	Replace **iye** with **iya**.	Don't do anything.	Replace **iye** with **iyu**.	Replace **iye** with **iyem**.	Replace **iye** with **ii**.
iya	Replace **iya** with **ii**.	Replace **iya** with **iyu**.	Replace **iya** with **ii**.	Replace **iya** with **iyej**.	Replace **iya** with **ii**.
j	Replace **j** with **ya**.	Replace **j** with **ya** if the noun is a living being; otherwise, don't do anything.	Replace **j** with **yu**.	Replace **j** with **yem**.	Replace **j** with **e**.

(continued)

Table 2-1 (continued)

If a Noun in Its Dictionary Form (Nominative Case) Ends In	To Form Genitive	To Form Accusative	To Form Dative	To Form Instrumental	To Form Prepositional
o	Replace -o with -a.	Don't do anything.	Replace -o with -u.	Replace -o with -om.	Replace -o with -ye.
ye	Replace -e with -ya.	Don't do anything.	Replace -ye with -yu.	Replace -ye with -yem.	Don't do anything.
ya	Replace -ya with -i.	Replace -ya with -yu.	Replace -ya with -ye.	Replace -ya with -yej.	Replace -ya with -ye.
Soft sign (')	If the noun is feminine, replace the soft sign with **i.** If the noun is masculine, replace the soft sign with **ya** and omit the last vowel of the word if it is **ye.**	If the noun is feminine, don't do anything. If the noun is masculine and a living being, replace the soft sign with **ya;** otherwise, don't do anything.	If the noun is feminine, replace the soft sign with **i.** If the noun is masculine, replace the soft sign with **yu** and omit the last vowel of the word if it is **ye.**	If the noun is feminine, replace the soft sign with **yu.** If the noun is masculine, replace the soft sign with **yem** and omit the last vowel of the word if it is **ye.**	If the noun is feminine, replace the soft sign with **i.** If the noun is masculine, replace the soft sign with **ye** and omit the last vowel of the word if it is **ye.**

Russian nouns in the nominative case (singular) never end in the letters **i, u, y, e,** or **yu.** A small number of nouns end in **yu,** but they're special cases and we deal with them as they come up.

This table may look kind of scary at first, but it's actually easy to use. Say you want to say "I bought my friend a car." The first part of the sentence is **ya kupil** (ya koo-*peel;* I bought). But what should you do with the nouns *car* and *friend?* In this sentence, **mashina** (muh-*shih*-nuh; car) is a direct object of the action expressed by the verb **kupil** (koo-*peel;* bought). That means you have to put **mashina** into the accusative case.

The next step is to find the appropriate ending in Table 2-1. You find this ending in the second row, third column. The table says to replace **a** with **u.**

Now what about **drug** (drook; friend)? Because *friend* is the indirect object of the sentence (the person to whom or for whom the action of the verb is directed), it takes the dative case in Russian. Table 2-1 indicates that if a noun ends in a consonant (as does **drug**), you form the dative case by adding the letter **u** to the final consonant. The correct form for **drug** in this sentence is **drugu** (*droog*-oo). So here's your complete sentence: **Ya kupil drugu mashinu** (yah koo-*peel droog*-oo muh-*shih*-noo; I bought my friend a car).

Putting plurals into their cases

As you probably guessed, Russian plural nouns take different endings depending on the case they're in. Table 2-2 shows you the rules for plural formation in the nominative case.

Table 2-2	Forming the Plural of Nouns in the Nominative Case
If a Noun in Its Dictionary Form (Nominative Case) Ends In	*To Form the Nominative Plural*
A consonant	Add **y.**
a	Replace **a** with **y.**
iye	Replace **iye** with **iya.**
iya	Replace **iya** with **ii.**
j	Replace **j** with **i.**
o	Replace **o** with **a.**
ye	Replace **ye** with **ya.**
ya	Replace **ya** with **i.**
Soft sign (')	Replace soft sign with **i** and if the last vowel is **ye,** omit it.

The rules in Table 2-2 have a few important exceptions. Some consonants, namely **zh, sh, sh', g, k,** and **kh,** are very touchy. They just don't tolerate the letter **y** after them and prefer an **i** instead. The plural of **kniga** (*knee-*guh; book) is **knigi** (*knee-*gee; books).

Changing plurals into the genitive case

Forming the plurals of nouns in the genitive case is a little trickier than in the other cases, so we deal with it first in Table 2-3.

Table 2-3	Forming the Plural of Nouns in the Genitive Case
If a Noun in Its Dictionary Form (Nominative Case) Ends In	**To Form Genitive Plural**
A consonant other than **zh, sh, sh', ch,** or **ts**	Add **ov: studyent** (stoo-*dyent;* male student) becomes **studyentov** (stoo-*dyen*-tuhf; male students).
zh, sh, sh', ch, or soft sign	Add **yej: klyuch** (klyuch; key) becomes **klyuchyej** (klu-*chyey;* keys).
ts	Add **yev: myesyats** (*mye*-seets; month) becomes **myesyatsyev** (*mye*-see-tsehf; months).
a	Drop the final **a.** If the resulting genitive plural form has two consonants at the end, the fill vowel **o** or **e** is often added between the consonants: **sosyedka** (sah-*s'ehd*-kuh; female neighbor) becomes **sosyedok** (sah-*s'eh*-duhk; female neighbors).
iye or **iya**	Replace **iye** or **iya** with **ij: stantsiya** (*stahn*-tsih-uh; station) becomes **stantsij** (*stahn*-tsihy; stations).
j	Replace the final **j** with **yov** if the ending is stressed, or with **yev** if the ending is not stressed: **popugaj** (puh-poo-*gahy;* parrot) becomes **popugayev** (puh-poo-*gah*-ehf; parrots).

(continued)

Table 2-3 *(continued)*

If a Noun in Its Dictionary Form (Nominative Case) Ends In	To Form Genitive Plural
o	Drop the **o**: **myesto** (*m'ehs*-tuh; place) becomes **myest** (m'ehst; places).
ye	Add **j**: **morye** (*moh*-ree; sea) becomes **moryej** (mah-*r'ehy*; seas).
Consonant + **ya**	Replace **ya** with the soft sign: **nyedyelya** (nee-*d'eh*-l'eh; week) becomes **nyedyel'** (nee-*d'ehl'*, weeks).

Now, try to apply Table 2-3 to a real-life situation. Imagine that your friend asks you **U tyebya yest' karandash?** (oo tee-*b'ah* yest' kuh-ruhn-*dahsh?*; Do you have a pencil?). You say that you have a lot of pencils, but the word *mnogo* (mnoh-guh; many/a lot of) requires that the noun used with it take the genitive plural form. In your sentence, the word **karandashi** (kuh-ruhn-dah-*shih*; pencils) should take the form of genitive plural. What does Table 2-3 say about the ending **sh?** That's right; you need to add the ending **yej.** You say **U myenya mnogo karandashyej** (oo mee-*n'ah* mnoh-guh kuh-ruhn-duh-*shehy*; I have many pencils).

Setting plurals into other cases

Table 2-4 shows how to form the plurals of nouns for all the other cases.

Table 2-4	Forming the Plural of Nouns in the Accusative, Dative, Instrumental, and Prepositional Cases			
If a Noun in Its Dictionary Form (Nominative Case) Ends In	To Form Accusative Plural	To Form Dative Plural	To Form Instrumental Plural	To Form Prepositional Plural
A consonant	If the noun is a living being, it looks just like the genitive plural (see Table 2-3); otherwise, it looks just like the nominative plural (see Table 2-2).	Add **am.**	Add **ami.**	Add **akh.**
a or ya	If the noun is a living being, it looks just like the genitive plural (see Table 2-3); otherwise, it looks just like the nominative plural (see Table 2-2).	Add **m.**	Add **mi.**	Add **kh.**

(continued)

Table 2-4 (continued)

If a Noun in Its Dictionary Form (Nominative Case) Ends In	To Form Accusative Plural	To Form Dative Plural	To Form Instrumental Plural	To Form Prepositional Plural
iye	Replace **iye** with **iya**, like the nominative plural (see Table 2-2).	Replace **ye** with **yam.**	Replace **iye** with **yami.**	Replace **ye** with **ye-kh.**
iya	Replace **iya** with **ii**, like the nominative plural (see Table 2-2).	Add **m.**	Add **mi.**	Add **kh.**
j	If the noun is a living being, it looks just like the genitive plural (see Table 2-3); otherwise, it looks just like the nominative plural (see Table 2-2).	Replace **j** with **yam.**	Replace **j** with **yami.**	Replace **j** with **yakh.**

If a Noun in Its Dictionary Form (Nominative Case) Ends In	To Form Accusative Plural	To Form Dative Plural	To Form Instrumental Plural	To Form Prepositional Plural
o	If the noun is a living being, it looks just like the genitive plural (see Table 2-3); otherwise, it looks just like the nominative plural (see Table 2-2).	Replace **o** with **am.**	Replace **o** with **ami.**	Replace **o** with **akh.**
ye	Replace **ye** with **ya,** like the nominative plural (see Table 2-2).	Replace **ye** with **yam.**	Add **yami.**	Replace **ye** with **yakh.**
A soft sign (')	If the noun is a living being, it looks just like the genitive plural (see Table 2-3); otherwise, it looks just like the nominative plural (see Table 2-2).	Replace the soft sign with **yam.**	Replace the soft sign with **yami** and omit the last vowel of the word if it is **ye.**	Replace the soft sign with **yakh.**

Picking out pronouns

Pronouns are words like *he*, *she*, and *it*. They're used in place of nouns to refer to someone or something that's already been mentioned.

Major Russian pronouns include the following:

- ✔ **ya** (ya; I)
- ✔ **ty** (tih; you [informal singular])
- ✔ **on** (ohn; he)
- ✔ **ona** (ah-*nah;* she)
- ✔ **my** (mih; we)
- ✔ **vy** (vih; you [formal singular and plural])

So what about *it?* In English, inanimate objects are usually referred to with the pronoun *it,* but in Russian, an inanimate object is always referred to with the pronoun corresponding to its grammatical gender. You translate the English pronoun into Russian with one of these pronouns:

- ✔ **on** (ohn), if the noun it refers to is masculine
- ✔ **ona** (ah-*nah*), if the noun it refers to is feminine
- ✔ **ono** (ah-*noh*), if the noun it refers to is neuter
- ✔ **oni** (ah-*nee*), if the noun it refers to is plural

For example, in the sentences **Eto moya mashina. Ona staraya** (*eh*-tuh mah-*ya* muh-*shih*-nuh ah-*nah stah*-ruh-yuh; That's my car. It's old), the pronoun *it* is translated as **ona,** because it refers to the Russian feminine noun **mashina.**

Placing basic pronouns into cases

Like nouns, Russian pronouns have different forms for all the cases. Table 2-5 shows the declension for pronouns.

Table 2-5 Declension of Russian Pronouns

Pronoun in the Nominative Case	Genitive	Accusative	Dative	Instrumental	Prepositional
ya (ya; I)	**myenya** (mee-*n'ah*; me)	**myenya** (mee-*n'ah*; me)	**mnye** (mn'eh; me)	**mnoj** (mnohy; me)	**mnye** (mn'eh; me)
ty (tih; you [informal singular])	**tyebya** (tee-*b'ah*; you)	**tyebya** (tee-*b'ah*; you)	**tyebye** (tee-*be*; you)	**toboj** (tah-*bohy*; you)	**tyebye** (tee-*b'eh*; you)
on (ohn; he or it)	**(n)yego** ([nee-*voh*] yee-*voh*; him or it)	**(n)yego** ([nee-*voh*] yee-*voh*; him or it)	**(n)yemu** ([nee-*moo*] yee-*moo*; him or it)	**(n)im** ([n]eem; him or it)	**nyom** (nyom; him or it)
ona (ah-*nah*; she or it)	**(n)yeyo** ([nee-*yoh*] yee-*yoh*; her or it)	**(n)yeyo** ([nee-*yoh*] yee-*yoh*; her or it)	**(n)yej** ([nehy] yehy; her or it)	**(n)yej** ([nehy] yehy; her or it)	**nej** (njey; her or it)

(continued)

Table 2-5 *(continued)*

Pronoun in the Nominative Case	Genitive	Accusative	Dative	Instrumental	Prepositional
ono (ah-*noh*; it)	**(n)yego** ([nee-*voh*] yee-*voh*; it)	**(n)yego** ([nee-*voh*] yee-*voh*; it)	**(n)yemu** ([nee-*moo*] yee-*moo*; it)	**(n)im** ([n]eem; it)	**(n)im** ([n]eem; it)
my (mih; we)	**nas** (nahs; us)	**nas** (nahs; us)	**nam** (nahm; us)	**nami** (*nah*-mee; us)	**nas** (nahs; us)
vy (vih; you [formal singular and plural])	**vas** (vahs; you)	**vas** (vahs; you)	**vam** (vahm; you)	**vami** (*vah*-mee; you)	**vas** (vahs; you)
oni (ah-*nee*; they)	**(n)ikh** ([n]eekh; them)	**(n)ikh** ([n]eekh; them)	**(n)im** ([n]eem; them)	**(n)imi** (*[n]ee*-mee; them)	**nikh** ([n]eekh; the ⌐

Surveying possessive pronouns

Possessive pronouns indicate ownership or possession and must always agree in number, gender, and case with the noun they're referring to. Table 2-6 shows you how to form the possessive pronouns in the nominative case, which is by far the case you'll use most.

Table 2-6	Forming Possessive Pronouns in the Nominative Case			
English Possessive Pronoun	**When It Modifies a Masculine Noun**	**When It Modifies a Feminine Noun**	**When It Modifies a Neuter Noun**	**When It Modifies a Plural Noun (All Genders)**
My/mine	**moj** (mohy)	**moya** (mah-*ya*)	**moyo** (mah-*yo*)	**moi** (mah-*ee*)
Your/yours (informal singular)	**tvoj** (tvohy)	**tvoya** (tvah-*ya*)	**tvoyo** (tvah-*yo*)	**tvoi** (tvah-*ee*)
His	**yego** (ee-*voh*)	**yego** (ee-*voh*)	**yego** (ee-*voh*)	**yego** (ee-*voh*)
Her/hers	**yeyo** (ee-*yo*)	**yeyo** (ee-*yo*)	**yeyo** (ee-*yo*)	**yeyo** (ee-*yo*)
Our/ours	**nash** (nahsh)	**nasha** (*nah*-shuh)	**nashye** (*nah*-sheh)	**nashi** (*nah*-shih)
Your/yours (formal singular and plural)	**vash** (vahsh)	**vasha** (*vah*-shuh)	**vashye** (*vah*-sheh)	**vashi** (*vah*-shih)
Their/theirs	**ikh** (eekh)	**ikh** (eekh)	**ikh** (eekh)	**ikh** (eekh)

Say you're getting ready to go out on the town and you notice you lost your favorite shirt. You want to say, "Where's my shirt?" Because **rubashka** (*roo-bahsh*-kuh; shirt) ends in **a**, it's a feminine noun. Because *my* modifies the feminine noun **rubashka**, it's written **moya** (mah-*ya;* my), according to Table 2-6. The phrase you want is **Gdye moya rubashka?** (gdye mah-*ya* roo-*bahsh*-kuh?; Where's my shirt?)

Investigating interrogative pronouns

Interrogative pronouns are question words like *who, whose,* and *which. Who* in Russian is **kto** (ktoh), and you're likely to hear or use this word in phrases like

- ✔ **Kto eto?** (ktoh *eh*-tuh?; Who is that?)
- ✔ **Kto on?** (ktoh ohn?; Who is he?)
- ✔ **Kto vy?** (ktoh vih?; Who are you?)

Kto changes its form depending on the case it's in. It becomes **kogo** (kah-*voh;* whom) in the genitive case, **kogo** (kah-*voh;* whom) in the accusative case, **komu** (koh-*moo;* whom) in the dative case, **kyem** (kyem; whom) in the instrumental case, and **kom** (kohm; whom) in the prepositional case. But you hear and use the basic nominative-case form **kto** in most situations. And just as in English, you use **kto** no matter what the gender of the noun is.

Whose in Russian is **chyej** (chehy), and *which* is **kakoj** (kuh-*kohy*). **Chyej** and **kakoj** change their endings depending on the gender, number, and case of the noun they modify. For now, you just need to know the nominative case endings in Table 2-7.

Table 2-7	Nominative Case Endings for *Chyej* (Whose) and *Kakoj* (Which)			
Interrogative Pronoun	*When It Modifies a Masculine Noun*	*When It Modifies a Feminine Noun*	*When It Modifies a Neuter Noun*	*When It Modifies a Plural Noun*
chyej (chehy; whose)	**chyej** (chehy)	**ch'ya** (ch'ya)	**ch'yo** (ch'yo)	**ch'i** (ch'yee)
kakoj (kuh-*kohy*, which)	**kakoj** (kuh-*kohy*)	**kakaya** (kuh-*kah*-yuh)	**kakoye** (kuh-*koh*-eh)	**kakiye** (kuh-*kee*-eh)

The question words **kogda** (kahg-*dah;* when), **gdye** (gdeh; where), and **chto** (shtoh; what) are also sometimes used as interrogative pronouns. The good news is that **kogda** and **gdye** never change their form. **Chto** changes its form for all cases.

Decorating Your Speech with Adjectives

Adjectives spice up your speech. An adjective is a word that describes, or modifies, a noun or a pronoun, like *good, nice, difficult,* or *hard.*

Always consenting: Adjective-noun agreement

A Russian adjective always agrees with the noun or pronoun it modifies in gender, number, and case. Table 2-8 shows how to change adjective endings in the nominative case, which is the case you're likely to see and use the most.

Table 2-8	Adjective Formation in the Nominative Case	
If an Adjective Modifies	*The Adjective Takes the Ending*	*Examples*
A masculine noun/pronoun	**oj//ij/yj**	**bol'shoj myach** (bahl'-*shohy* m'ahch; big ball)
		sinij pidzhak (*see*-neey peed-*zhahk;* blue jacket)
		krasivyj mal'chik (kruh-*see*-vihy *mahl'*-cheek; beautiful boy)
A feminine noun/pronoun	**aya/yaya**	**bol'shaya kniga** (bahl'-*shah*-uh *knee*-guh; big book)
		sinyaya shuba (*see*-nee-uh *shoo*-buh; blue fur coat)
		krasivaya rubashka (krah-*see*-vuh-uh roo-*bahsh*-kuh; beautiful shirt)
A neuter noun	**oye/yeye**	**bol'shoye zhivotnoye** (bahl'-*shoh*-eh zhih-*voht*-nuh-eh; big animal)
		sinyeye okno (*see*-nee-eh ahk-*noh;* blue window)
		krasivoye myesto (krah-*see*-vuh-eh *myes*-tuh; beautiful place)

If an Adjective Modifies	The Adjective Takes the Ending	Examples
A plural noun	**yye/iye**	**bol'shyye zhivotnyye** (bahl'-*shih*-eh zhee-*voht*-nih-eh; big animals)
		siniye okna (see-nee-eh *ohk*-nuh; blue windows)
		krasivyye myesta (krah-*see*-vih-eh mees-*tah;* beautiful places)

A lot in common: Putting adjectives into other cases

Table 2-9 shows how to change adjective endings for all the cases other than nominative. (Work with Table 2-8 to figure out which particular ending to use in each case.) Notice how masculine and neuter nouns take the same endings in the genitive, dative, instrumental, and prepositional cases. The feminine endings are the same for all cases except accusative. And the plural genitive and plural prepositional endings are the same.

Table 2-9 Adjective Declension in the Genitive, Accusative, Instrumental, and Prepositional Cases

If the Adjective Modifies	To Form Genitive	To Form Accusative	To Form Dative	To Form Instrumental	To Form Prepositional
A masculine noun	Replace **oj/ij/yj** with **ogo/yego/ogo.**	If the noun is a living being, it looks just like the genitive; otherwise, it looks just like the nominative (see Table 2-8).	Replace **oj/ij/yj** with **omu/yemu/omu.**	Replace **oj/ij/yj** with **ym/im/ym.**	Replace **oj/ij/yj** with **om/im/om.**
A feminine noun	Replace **aya/yaya** with **oj/yej/oj.**	Replace **aya/yaya** with **uyu/yuyu/uyu.**	Replace **aya/yaya** with **oj/yej/oj.**	Replace **aya/yaya** with **oj/yej/oj.**	Replace **aya/yaya** with **oj/yej/oj.**
A neuter noun	Replace **oye/yeye** with **ogo/yego.**	It looks just like the nominative (see Table 2-8).	Replace **oye/yeye** with **omu/yemu.**	Replace **oye/yeye** with **ym/im.**	Replace **oye/yeye** with **om/im.**
A plural noun	Replace **yye/iye** with **ykh/ikh.**	If the noun is a living being, it looks just like the genitive; otherwise, it looks just like the nominative (see Table 2-8).	Replace **yye/iye** with **ym/im.**	Replace **yye/iye** with **ymi/imi.**	Replace **yye/iye** with **ykh/ikh.**

Nowhere to be found: The lack of articles in Russian

The English words *the, a,* and *an* are called articles. You use articles all the time in English, but these words don't exist in Russian, so you don't need to worry about how to say them. When you want to say *the, a,* or *an,* all you have to do is say the noun you mean. "The store" and "a store" in Russian are simply **magazin** (muh-guh-*zeen; literally:* store). "The girl" and "a girl" are simply **dye-vushka** (*dyeh*-voosh-kuh; *literally*: girl).

Adding Action with Verbs

A Russian verb carries loads of important information. It can reveal whether an action was completed or resulted in something and whether the action occurs on a regular basis or is a one-time event. Russian verbs also reveal the number (and, in the past tense, the gender) of the person or thing performing the action.

Spotting infinitives

Spotting Russian infinitives is easy, because they usually end in a **t'** as in **chitat'** (chee-*taht';* to read), **govorit'** (guh-vah-*reet';* to speak), and **vidyet'** (*veed*-yet'; to see).

Some Russian verbs (which are usually irregular) take the infinitive endings **ti** as in **idti** (ee-*tee;* to walk) and **ch'** as in **moch'** (mohch'; to be able to).

Living in the present tense

Russian verbs have only one present tense. Like English verbs, Russian verbs *conjugate* (change their form) so that they always agree in person and number with the subject of the sentence. To conjugate most Russian

verbs in the present tense, you drop the infinitive
ending **t'** and replace it with one of the six endings in
Table 2-10.

Table 2-10	Forming the Present Tense of Verbs	
Subject of Sentence	*Drop the Infinitive Verb Ending (t') and Replace It With*	*Example*
ya (ya; I)	**yu**	**ya rabotayu** (ya ruh-*boh*-tuh-yu; I work or I am working)
ty (tih; you [informal singular])	**yesh'**	**ty rabotayesh'** (tih ruh-*boh*-tuh-ehsh'; You work or you are working)
on/ona/ono (ohn/ah-nah/ah-noh; he/she/it)	**yet**	**on rabotayet** (ohn ruh-*boh*-tuh-eht; He works or he is working)
my (mih; we)	**yem**	**my rabotayem** (mih ruh-*boh*-tuh-ehm; We work or we are working)
vy (vih; you [formal singular and plural])	**yetye**	**vy rabotayetye** (vih ruh-*boh*-tuh-eh-tye; You work or you are working)
oni (ah-*nee*; they)	**yut**	**oni rabotayut** (ah-*nee* ruh-*boh*-tuh-yut; They work or they are working)

Always check the dictionary for clues to anything peculiar in verb conjugations.

Keep it simple: Forming the past tense

To form the past tense of a Russian verb, all you need
to do is drop the infinitive ending **t'** and replace it
with one of four endings in Table 2-11.

Table 2-11 Forming the Past Tense of Verbs

If the Subject of the Sentence Is	Drop the Infinitive Ending t' and Replace It With	Example
Masculine singular	l	**on rabotal** (ohn ruh-*boh*-tuhl; He worked)
Feminine singular	la	**ona rabotala** (ah-nah ruh-*boh*-tuh-luh; She worked)
Neuter singular	lo	**ono rabotalo** (ah-noh ruh-*boh*-tuh-luh; It worked)
Plural	li	**oni rabotali** (ah-*nee* ruh-*boh*-tuh-lee; They worked)

Past again: Perfective or imperfective?

English expresses past events either through the past-simple tense (I ate yesterday), which simply states a fact, or the present-perfect tense (I have eaten already), which emphasizes the result of the action. Russian verbs do something similar by using what's called *verbal aspect:* perfective and imperfective.

Up to this point, we've been withholding some very essential information from you: Every English verb is represented by two Russian verbs: its imperfective equivalent and a perfective counterpart. Usually, the imperfective is listed first, as in this example:

To read — **chitat'** (chee-*taht'*)/**prochitat'** (pruh-chee-*taht'*)

Chitat' is the imperfective infinitive, and **prochitat'** is the perfective infinitive. You form the perfective aspect by adding the prefix **pro** to the imperfective infinitive. However, sometimes the perfective aspect of a verb looks quite different from the imperfective aspect, so always check the dictionary.

The imperfective aspect form of the verb emphasizes the fact of an action in the past or to express habitual or repeated action in the past. The perfective aspect emphasizes the result or completion of the action. You also use the perfective aspect of a verb if you want to emphasize a single, momentary event that took place in the past, such as breaking a plate.

If you tell someone **Ya pisal ryezyumye tsyelyj dyen'** (ya pee-*sahl* ree-z'oo-*meh tseh* -lihy d'ehn'; I was writing my résumé all day), you use the past tense imperfective form of the verb **pisat',** because your emphasis is on the fact of writing, not on the completion of the task. If you finished writing your résumé, you use the past tense perfective form of the verb, because your emphasis is on the completion of the action: **Ya napisal ryesyumye** (ya nuh-pee-*sahl* ree-z'oo-*meh;* I have written my résumé).

Planning for the future tense

To describe an action that will take place in the future, Russian uses the future tense. Although English has many different ways to talk about the future, Russian has only two: the *future imperfective* and the *future perfective*.

You use the future imperfective when you want to emphasize the fact that something will happen or be happening in the future, but you don't necessarily want to emphasize the result or completion of an action. You use the future perfective to emphasize result or completion of an action.

To form the future imperfective, you use the future tense form of the verb **byt'** (biht'; to be) plus the imperfective infinitive. This combination translates into "will/will be." Table 2-12 shows the conjugation of the verb **byt'** in the future tense.

Table 2-12	Conjugation of *Byt'* in the Future Tense
Pronoun	**Correct Form of Byt'**
ya (I)	**budu** (*boo*-doo)
ty (you [informal singular])	**budyesh'** (*boo*-d'ehsh')
on/ona/ono (he/she/it)	**budyet** (*boo*-d'eht)
my (we)	**budyem** (*boo*-d'ehm)
vy (you [formal singular and plural])	**budyetye** (*boo*-d'eh-t'eh)
oni (they)	**budut** (*boo*-doot)

If you want to say "I will read (but not necessarily finish reading) the article," you use the **ya** (I) form of the verb **byt'** plus the imperfective infinitive **chitat'** (chee-*taht';* to read): **Ya budu chitat' stat'yu** (ya *boo*-doo chee-*taht'* staht'-*yu*).

To form the future perfective, you simply conjugate the perfective form of the verb, as in **Ya prochitayu stat'yu syegodnya** (ya pruh-chee-*tah*-yu staht'-*yu* see-*vohd*-n'uh; I'll read/finish reading the article today). In other words, you use the ending **yu** for **ya** (I) as you do in the present tense. See the previous section for more about perfective verbs.

Using the unusual verb byt' (to be)

Russian has no present tense of the verb *to be*. To say "I'm happy," you just say **Ya schastliv** (ya sh'ahs-leef; *literally:* I happy). To say "That's John," you just say **Eto Dzhon** (*eh*-tuh dzhohn; *literally*: That John). The being verbs *am, are,* and *is* are implicitly understood in the present tense.

To express the verb *to be* in the past tense, you need
to use the proper past-tense form of the verb **byt':**

- ✔ **byl** (bihl; was), if the subject is a masculine singular noun

- ✔ **byla** (bih-*lah;* was), if the subject is a feminine
  singular noun

- ✔ **bylo** (*bih*-luh; was), if the subject is a neuter singular noun

- ✔ **byli** (*bih*-lee; was), if the subject is a plural noun
  or if the subject is **vy** (vih; you [formal singular])

To express the verb to be in the future tense, you
have to use the correct form of the verb **byt'** in the
future tense. (For conjugation, refer to Table 2-12.) To
say "I will be happy," you say **Ya budu schastliv**
(ya *boo*-doo *sh'ahs*-leef), and for "I will be there," you
say **Ya budu tam** (ya *boo*-doo tahm).

Chapter 3

Numerical Gumbo: Counting of All Kinds

. . . .

In This Chapter

▶ Counting to 20

▶ Telling time

▶ Counting the days

▶ Spending money

. . . .

*T*his chapter gives you a rundown of all the numbers, dates, and money phrases you need to know to navigate your daily routine in Russian.

Counting in Russian

The harsh truth is that each Russian number changes its form for all six cases! (See Chapter 2 for more on cases.) But unless you plan to spend a lot of time at mathematics or accounting conferences conducted in Russian, you won't find yourself in many practical situations in which you need to know all the different forms. So we give you all the numbers you need to know only in the nominative case.

Numbers 0 through 9

These are the numbers you'll probably use most often:

- ✔ **nol'** (nohl'; zero)
- ✔ **odin** (ah-*deen;* one)
- ✔ **dva** (dvah; two)
- ✔ **tri** (tree; three)
- ✔ **chyetyrye** (chee-*tih*-r'eh; four)
- ✔ **pyat'** (p'aht'; five)
- ✔ **shyest'** (shehst'; six)
- ✔ **syem'** (s'ehm'; seven)
- ✔ **vosyem'** (*voh*-s'ehm'; eight)
- ✔ **dyevyat'** (*d'eh*-v'uht'; nine)

But wait! You have to use a few rules when you use these numbers:

- ✔ **The number one followed by a noun:** For masculine nouns, you say **odin** followed by the noun as in **odin chyelovyek** (ah-*deen* chee-lah-*v'ehk;* one man). If the noun is feminine you say **odna** as in **odna dyevushka** (ahd-*nah d'eh*-voosh-kuh; one girl). And if the noun is neuter you say **odno** as in **odno okno** (ahd-*noh* ahk-*noh;* one window).

- ✔ **The number two followed by a noun:** For masculine or neuter nouns, you say **dva,** and if the noun is feminine, **dva** becomes **dvye.** After the numeral two, you have to put the noun into the genitive case singular as in **dva chyelovyeka** (dvah chee-lah-*v'eh*-kuh; two men), **dva okna** (dvah ahk-*nah;* two windows), and **dvye dyevushki** (dv'eh *d'eh*-voosh-kee; two girls).

- ✔ **The numbers three and four followed by a noun:** Like the numeral **dva** (dvah; two), **tri** (tree; three) and **chyetyrye** (chee-*tih*-r'eh; four) also require the noun used after them to be put into the genitive singular. Unlike **odin** and **dva,** these numbers don't change their form depending on the gender of the noun they refer to.

✔ **The numbers five through nine followed by a noun:** When you use any noun after the numerals five through nine, you must put the noun into the genitive plural case, as in the phrase **pyat' dyevushyek** (p'aht *d'eh*-voo-shehk; five girls) and **syem' mal'chikov** (s'ehm' *mahl*-chee-kuhf; seven boys). Unlike **odin** and **dva,** these numbers don't change their form depending on the gender of the noun they're used with.

Numbers 10 through 19

The following are the numbers 10 through 19:

✔ **dyesyat'** (*d'eh*-s'uht'; 10)

✔ **odinnadtsat'** (ah-*dee*-nuht-tsuht'; 11)

✔ **dvyenadtsat'** (dvee-*naht*-tsuht'; 12)

✔ **trinadtsat'** (tree-*naht*-tsuht'; 13)

✔ **chyetyrnadtsat'** (chee-*tihr*-nuht-tsuht'; 14)

✔ **pyatnadtsat'** (peet-*naht*-tsuht'; 15)

✔ **shyestnadtsat'** (shees-*naht*-tsuht'; 16)

✔ **syemnadtsat'** (seem-*naht*-tsuht'; 17)

✔ **vosyemnadtsyat'** (vuh-seem-*naht*-tsuht'; 18)

✔ **dyevyatnadtsat'** (dee-veet-*naht*-tsuht'; 19)

Nouns following all these numerals take the genitive plural.

First, Second: Ordinal Numbers

Ordinal numbers are numbers like first, second, and third. We list the first 20 here:

✔ **pyervyj** (*p'ehr*-vihy; 1st)

✔ **vtoroj** (ftah-*rohy;* 2nd)

✔ **tryetij** (*tr'eh*-teey; 3rd)

✔ **chyetvyertyj** (cheet-*v'ohr*-tihy; 4th)

- **pyatyj** (*p'ah*-tihy; 5th)
- **shyestoj** (shees-*tohy;* 6th)
- **syed'moj** (seed'-*mohy;* 7th)
- **vos'moj** (vahs'-*mohy;* 8th)
- **dyevyatyj** (dee-*v'ah*-tihy; 9th)
- **dyesyatyj** (dee-*s'ah*-tihy; 10th)
- **odinnadtsatyj** (ah-*dee*-nuht-suh-tihy; 11th)
- **dvyennadtsatyj** (dvee-*naht*-suh-tihy; 12th)
- **trinadtsatyj** (tree-*naht*-suh-tihy; 13th)
- **chyetyrnadtsatyj** (chee-*tihr*-nuht-suh-tihy; 14th)
- **pyatnadtsatyj** (peet-*naht*-suh-tihy; 15th)
- **shyestnadtsatyj** (shees-*naht*-suh-tihy; 16th)
- **syemnadtsatyj** (seem-*naht*-suh-tihy; 17th)
- **vosyem'nadtsatyj** (vuh-seem-*naht*-suh-tihy; 18th)
- **dyevyatnadtsatyj** (dee-veet-*naht*-suh-tihy; 19th)
- **dvadtsatyj** (dvuht-*sah*-tihy; 20th)

The Clock's Ticking: Telling Time

When you go out and have fun, **vryemya** (*vr'eh*-m'uh; time) is crucial. In the following sections, we help you state and ask for time and specify times of the day and days of the week.

Counting the hours

Just like in Europe, Russia uses the 24-hour system for each day. Instead of 3 p.m., you may hear the phrase **pyatnadtsdat' chasov** (peet-*naht*-tsuht' chuh-*sohf;* 15 o'clock [*literally:* 15 hours]). Russians use this form of time-telling for all kinds of official messages: schedules, radio and TV announcements, working hours, and so on.

In everyday situations, however, most people use the first 12 numerals to indicate both a.m. and p.m. hours.

If you want to indicate "a.m." when using the 12-hour system, you say **utra** (oot-*rah; literally:* in the morning) after the time; you say **dnya** (dn'ah; *literally:* in the day) after the time to indicate "p.m." So 5 a.m. would be **pyat' chasov utra** (p'aht' chuh-*sohf* oot-*rah*), and 5 p.m. would be **pyat' chasov dnya** (p'aht' chuh-*sohf* dn'ah). When you're using the 24-hour system, you don't have to add the words **utra** or **dnya.**

Saying "o'clock" in Russian is kind of tricky. These simple rules, however, should help you translate this word into Russian:

- ✔ If the time is one o'clock, you just use the word **chas,** as in **Syejchas chas** (see-*chahs* chahs; It's one o'clock). You don't even have to say **odin** (ah-*deen;* one) before the word **chas.**

- ✔ After the numeral **dvadtsat' odin** (*dvaht*-tsuht' ah-*deen;* 21), use the word **chas** (chahs; o'clock), as in **Syejchas dvadtsat' odin chas** (see-chahs *dvaht*-tsuht' ah-*deen* chahs; It's 21 o'clock), or in other words, 9 p.m.

- ✔ After the numbers **dva** (dvah; 2), **tri** (tree; 3), **chyetyrye** (chee-*tih*-ree; 4), **dvadtsat' dva** (*dvaht*-tsuht' dvah; 22), **dvadtsat' tri** (*dvaht*-tsuht' tree; 23), and **dvadtsat' chyetyrye** (*dvaht*-tsuht' chee-*tih*-ree; 24), use the word **chasa** (chuh-*sah;* o'clock), as in **Syejchas tri chasa** (see-*chahs* tree chuh-*sah;* It's 3 o'clock).

- ✔ With all other numerals indicating time, use the word **chasov** (chuh-*sohf;* o'clock), as in **Syejchas pyat chasov** (see-*chahs* p'aht' chuh-*sohf;* It's five o'clock).

One final tip: To say "noon" in Russian, you just say **poldyen'** (*pohl*-d'ehn'; *literally:* half-day). When you want to say "midnight," you say **polnoch'** (*pohl*-nuhch; *literally:* half night).

Marking the minutes

In the following sections, we show you different ways to keep time by expressing **minuta** (mee-*noo*-tuh; minute) time increments in Russian.

On the half-hour

The easiest way to state the time by the half-hour in Russian is just to add the words **tridtsat' minut** (*treet*-tsuht' mee-*noot;* 30 minutes) to the hour: **Syejchas dva chasa tridtsat' minut** (see-*chahs* dvah chuh-*sah treet*-tsuht' mee-*noot;* It's 2:30). In more conversational speech, it's common to drop the words **chasa** and **minut** and just say **Syejchas dva tridtsat'** (see-*chahs* dvah *treet*-tsuht'; It's 2:30).

However, you may hear other ways of talking about half-hour increments, such as **Syejchas polovina vtorogo** (see-*chahs* puh-lah-*vee*-nuh ftah-*roh*-vuh; It's half past one [*literally:* It's half of two]).

The word **polovina** literally means "half of," not "half past." What you're really saying is "half of" whatever the next hour is. Therefore, 1:30 in Russian is literally "half of two," or **polovina vtorogo,** and 2:30 is literally "half of three," or **polovina tryet'yego.**

In a phrase like **Syejchas polovina vtorogo,** the Russian word used to indicate the hour **(vtorogo)** is the genitive form of the ordinal number **vtoroj** (ftah-*rohy;* second).

On the quarter hour

To indicate a quarter after an hour, Russian typically uses the phrase **pyatnadtsat' minut** (peet-*naht*-tsuht' mee-*noot;* 15 minutes). To say it's 5:15, you just say:

> **Syejchas pyat' chasov pyatnadtsat' minut** (see-*chahs* p'aht' chuh-*sohf* peet-*naht*-tsuht' mee-*noot; literally:* It's 5 hours 15 minutes)

To be more conversational, you can drop **chasov** and **minut** and say **Syejchas pyat' pyatnadtsat'** (see-*chahs* p'aht' peet-*naht*-tsuht'; It's 5:15).

To indicate a quarter to an hour, use the word **byez** (b'ehs; without) with **pyatnadtsati** and the hour, as in:

> **Syejchas byez pyatnadtsati pyat'** (see-*chahs* bees peet-*naht*-tsuh-tee p'aht'; It's 4:45 [*literally:* It's 5 without 15 minutes])

Other times before or after the hour

To state times that aren't on the half- or quarter-hour, you can simply use the construction **Syejchas . . . chasa** (or **chasov**) + **. . . minut**, as in **Syejchas chyetyrye chasa dyesyat' minut** (see-*chahs* chee-*tih*-ree chuh-*sah* d'*eh*-seet' mee-*noot;* It's 4:10). For more conversational speech, you can also drop the words **chasa** (or **chasov**) and **minut** and just say **Syejchas chyetyrye dyesyat'** (see-*chahs* chee-*tih*-r'eh d'*eh*-s'uht').

To express times right before the hour, you use the construction **Syejchas byez** plus the numbers indicating the minutes and the next hour. "It's ten to five" is **Syejchas byez dyesyati pyat** (see-*chahs* bees dee-see-*tee* p'aht'; *literally:* It's five minus ten minutes). In this construction, it's common to drop the words **minut** (minutes) and **chasov** (hours) after the numerals indicating the time.

 When using this expression, you must always remember to put the numeral after the word **byez** into the genitive case. Here are the genitive-case forms of the numerals you most often use with this expression:

- ✔ **odnoj** (ahd-*nohy;* 1)
- ✔ **dvukh** (dvookh; 2)
- ✔ **tryokh** (tryokh; 3)
- ✔ **chyetyryokh** (chee-tih-*r'ohkh;* 4)
- ✔ **pyati** (pee-*tee;* 5)
- ✔ **dyesyati** (dee-see-*tee;* 10)
- ✔ **pyat'nadtsati** (peet-*naht*-tsuh-tee; 15)
- ✔ **dvadtsati** (dvaht-tsuh-*tee;* 20)
- ✔ **dvadtsati pyati** (dvuht-tsuh-*tee* pee-*tee;* 25)

Asking for the time

To ask what time it is, you say **Skol'ko syejchas vryemyeni?** (*skohl'*-kuh see-*chahs vr'eh*-m'eh-nee?; What time is it?) If you ask a passerby in public, you may want to begin this question with the polite phrase **Izvinitye pozhalujsta . . .** (eez-vee-*nee*-t'eh pah-*zhah*-luh-stuh . . . ; Excuse me, please . . .) or **Skazhitye pozhalujsta . . .** (skuh-*zhih*-t'eh pah-*zhah*-luh-stuh . . . ; Could you please tell me . . .).

To ask at what time something will happen or has happened, use the phrases **Kogda** (*kahg*-dah; when) or **V kakoye vryemya . . .** (f kuh-*koh*-ee *vr'eh*-m'uh . . . ; At what time . . .).

Knowing the times of the day

People all over the world seem to agree on three main time periods: **utro** (*oo*-truh; morning), **dyen'** (d'ehn'; afternoon), and **vyechyer** (*v'eh*-chehr; evening). **Noch'** (nohch; night) is the time when most people sleep. To state that something happens within these time periods, use these phrases:

- **utrom** (*oo*-truhm; in the morning)
- **dnyom** (dn'ohm; in the afternoon)
- **vyechyerom** (*v'eh*-cheh-ruhm; in the evening)
- **noch'yu** (*nohch*-yu; late at night or early in the morning)

Although English uses the prepositional phrase "in + time of the day" to indicate times of the day, in Russian you put the words **utro, dyen', vyechyer,** and **noch'** in instrumental case. Also note that the word **dyen'** drops the letter **ye** in the process and becomes **dnyom** rather than **denyom.** Nouns sometimes have this habit of "losing" letters in the process of declining for cases in Russian.

Monday, Tuesday: Weekdays

To indicate days of the week, use these Russian words:

- ✔ **ponyedyel'nik** (puh-nee-*d'ehl'*-neek; Monday)
- ✔ **vtornik** (*ftohr*-neek; Tuesday)
- ✔ **sryeda** (sree-*dah;* Wednesday)
- ✔ **chyetvyerg** (cheet-*v'ehrk;* Thursday)
- ✔ **pyatnitsa** (*p'aht*-nee-tsuh; Friday)
- ✔ **subbota** (soo-*boh*-tuh; Saturday)
- ✔ **voskryesyen'ye** (vuhs-kree-*s'ehn'*-ye; Sunday)

If somebody asks you what day of the week it is, he says: **Kakoj syegodnya dyen'?** (kuh-*kohy* see-*vohd*-n'uh d'ehn'?; What day is it today?) To answer this question, you say **Syegodnya** plus the day of the week. For example: **Syegodnya ponyedyel'nik** (see-*vohd-n'uh* puh-nee-*d'ehl'*-neek; It's Monday today). It's that simple!

To say that something happens, happened, or will happen on a certain day, you need to add the preposition **v,** and you put the word denoting the day of the week into the accusative case. (For more on cases, see Chapter 2.)

- ✔ **v ponyedyel'nik** (f puh-nee-*d'ehl'*-neek; on Monday)
- ✔ **vo vtornik** (vah *ftohr*-neek; on Tuesday)
- ✔ **v sryedu** (f *sr'eh*-doo; on Wednesday)
- ✔ **v chyetvyerg** (f cheet-*v'ehrk;* on Thursday)
- ✔ **v pyatnitsu** (f *p'aht*-nee-tsuh; on Friday)
- ✔ **v subbotu** (f soo-*boh*-too; on Saturday)
- ✔ **v voskryesyen'ye** (v vuhs-kree-*s'ehn'*-ee; on Sunday)

You may wonder why some of the days change in the accusative case, while others don't. The explanation is simple: Masculine nouns denoting inanimate objects don't change their form in accusative case and retain their nominative (dictionary) form.

Other phrases related to the days of the week include

- ✔ **dyen'** (d'ehn'; day)
- ✔ **syegodnya** (see-*vohd*-n'uh; today)
- ✔ **syegodnya utrom** (see-*vohd*-n'uh *oo*-truhm; this morning)
- ✔ **syegodnya vyechyerom** (see-*vohd*-n'uh *v'eh*-ch'eh-ruhm; this evening)
- ✔ **nyedyelya** (nee-*d'eh*-l'uh; week)

Talking about time relative to the present

Just as in English, Russian has lots of phrases to talk about a certain time in the past or future that relates to the present moment. Some time-related words that you may hear or say often in Russian are

- ✔ **syejchas** (see-*chahs;* now)
- ✔ **skoro** (*skoh*-ruh; soon)
- ✔ **pozdno** (*pohz*-nuh; late)
- ✔ **pozzhye** (*poh*-zheh; later)
- ✔ **rano** (*rah*-nuh; early)
- ✔ **ran'shye** (*rahn'*-sheh; earlier)
- ✔ **vchyera** (fchee-*rah;* yesterday)
- ✔ **pozavchyera** (puh-zuhf-ch'eh-*rah;* the day before yesterday)
- ✔ **zavtra** (*zahf*-truh; tomorrow)
- ✔ **poslyezavtra** (*poh*-sl'eh-*zahf*-truh; the day after tomorrow)

If you want to express that something will happen in a week, a month, or a year, you use **chyeryez** plus the accusative form of either **nyedyelya** (nee-d'yh-l'un; week), **myesyats** (m'eh-seets; month), or **god** (goht; year):

> ✔ **chyeryez nyedyelyu** (*cheh*-r'ehz nee-*d'eh*-l'oo; in a week)

> ✔ **chyeryez myesyats** (*cheh*-reez *m'eh*-s'uhts; in a month)

> ✔ **chyeryez god** (*cheh*-r'ehz goht; in a year)

To say that something happened last week, month, or year, you say

> ✔ **na proshloj nyedyele** (nuh *prohsh*-luhy nee-*d'eh*-l'eh; last week)

> ✔ **v proshlom myesyatsye** (v *prohsh*-luhm *m'eh*-see-tseh; last month)

> ✔ **v proshlom godu** (v *prohsh*-luhm gah-*doo;* last year)

Checking Your Calendar

September, April, June, and November may all have 30 days, but here's some more important things to know about your calendar.

Recognizing the names of the months

Here's a list of the **myesyatsy** (m'eh-see-tsih; months):

> ✔ **yanvar'**(yeen-*vahr';* January)

> ✔ **fyevral'** (feev-*rahl';* February)

> ✔ **mart** (mahrt; March)

> ✔ **apryel'**(uhp-*r'ehl';* April)

> ✔ **maj** (mahy; May)

> ✔ **iyun'**(ee-*yun';* June)

- **iyul'** (ee-*yul'*; July)

- **avgust** (*ahv*-goost; August)

- **syentyabr'** (seen-*t'ahbr'*; September)

- **oktyabr'** (ahk-*t'ahbr'*; October)

- **noyabr'** (nah-*yahbr'*; November)

- **dyekabr'** (dee-*kahbr'*; December)

When you want to say a **chislo** (chees-*loh*; date) in Russian, you need to put the ordinal number indicating the day in the form of neuter gender and the name of the month in the genitive case, as in:

- **Syegodnya pyatoye oktyabrya** (see-*vohd*-n'uh p'*ah*-tuh-eh uhk-teeb-*r'ah;* Today is October 5).

- **Zavtra dyesyatoye iyulya** (*zahf*-truh dee-*s'ah*-tuh-eh ee-*yu*-l'uh; Tomorrow is June 10).

- **Poslyezavtra dvadtstat' chyetvyortoye marta** (*pohs*-lee-*zahf*-truh *dvaht*-tsuht' cheet-*v'ohr*-tuh-eh *mahr*-tuh; The day after tomorrow is March 24).

Saying the year

To indicate a year, you begin with the century, as in **tysyacha dyevyatsot** (*tih*-see-chuh dee-veet-*soht;* 19 [*literally:* 1,900]) for the 20th century or **dvye tysyachi** (dv'eh *tih*-see-chee; 2,000) for the 21st century. Then, to state the number indicating the year, use the corresponding ordinal number, as in:

- **tysyacha dyevyatsot pyat'dyesyat' vos'moj god** (*tih*-see-chuh dee-veet-*soht* pee-dee-*s'aht* vahs'-*mohy* goht; 1958 [*literally:* 1,958th year])

- **dvye tysyachi syed'moj god** (dv'eh *tih*-see-chee seed'-*mohy* goht; 2007 [*literally:* 2,007th year])

Note that in indicating a year, Russian, unlike English, actually uses the word **god** (goht; year). The word god has two plural forms: the regular **gody** (*goh*-dih; years) and the irregular **goda** (gah-*dah;* years). A very subtle stylistic difference exists between the two, so don't hesitate to use both or the one you like better.

To indicate when a certain event took, takes, or will take place, use preposition **v** + the year in the prepositional case + **godu** (gah-*doo;* year), as in:

> **v tysyacha dyevyatsot pyat'dyesyat vos'mom godu** (v *tih*-see-chuh dee-veet-*soht* pee-dee-*s'aht* vahs'-*mohm* gah-*doo;* in 1958 [*literally:* in the 1,958th year])

To indicate the year in which an event takes place, you only have to put the last ordinal numeral describing the year into the prepositional case.

Surveying the seasons

Russia has some beautiful **vryemyena goda** (vree-mee-*nah goh*-duh; seasons [*literally:* times of the year]). Here they are:

- ✔ **zima** (zee-*mah;* winter)
- ✔ **vyesna** (vees-*nah;* spring)
- ✔ **lyeto** (*l'eh*-tuh; summer)
- ✔ **osyen'** (*oh*-s'ehn'; fall)

A popular Russian song says **V prirodye plokhoj pogody nye byvayet** (v pree-*roh*-d'eh plah-*khohy* pah-*goh*-dih nee bih-*vah*-eht; Nature doesn't have bad weather). This line is another way of saying that every **vryemya goda** (*vr'eh*-m'uh *goh*-duh; season [*literally:* time of the year]) has its own beauty.

Money, Money, Money

The official Russian currency is the **rubl** (roobl', ruble). Much like a dollar equals 100 cents, one **rubl'** equals 100 **kopyejki** (kah-*p'ehy*-kee; kopecks).

To talk about different numbers of rubles, you need to use different cases, such as **dva rublya** (dvah roob-*l'ah;* 2 rubles) in the genitive singular, **pyat' rublyej** (p'aht' roob-*l'ehy;* 5 rubles) in the genitive plural, and **dvadtsat' odin rubl'** (*dvaht*-tsuht' ah-*deen* roobl'; 21 rubles) in the nominative singular.

Changing money

Big Russian cities are saturated with **punkty obmyena** (*poonk*-tih ahb-*m'eh*-nuh; currency-exchange offices), which can also be called **obmyen valyuty** (ahb-*m'ehn* vuh-*lyu*-tih). You can usually find a **punkt obmyena** in any hotel. The best **kurs obmyena valyuty** (koors ahb-*m'eh*-nuh vuh-*l'oo*-tih; exchange rate), however, is offered by **banki** (*bahn*-kee; banks).

Some handy phrases to use when you exchange currency include

- ✔ **Ya khochu obmyenyat' dyen'gi.** (ya khah-*choo* uhb-mee-*n'aht' d'ehn'*-gee; I want to exchange money.)

- ✔ **Ya khochu obmyenyat' dollary na rubli.** (ya khah-*choo* uhb-mee-*n'aht' doh*-luh-rih nuh roob-*lee;* I want to exchange dollars for rubles.)

- ✔ **Kakoj kurs obmyena?** (kuh-*kohy* koors ahb-*m'eh*-nuh?; What is the exchange rate?)

- ✔ **Nado platit' komissiyu?** (*nah*-duh pluh-*teet'* kah-*mee*-see-yu?; Do I have to pay a fee?)

Heading to the ATM

The fastest way to access your account is the **banko-mat** (buhn-kah-*maht;* ATM). **Bankomaty** (buhn-kah-*mah*-tih; ATMs) are less ubiquitous in small cities; they're usually found in banks.

Here's your guide to the phrases you see on the **bankomat** screen:

✔ **vstav'tye kartu** (*fstahf'*-t'eh *kahr*-too; insert the card)

✔ **vvyeditye PIN-kod** (vee-*dee*-t'eh peen-*koht;* enter your PIN)

✔ **vvyeditye summu** (vvee-*dee*-t'eh *soo*-moo; enter the amount)

✔ **snyat' nalichnyye** (sn'aht' nuh-*leech*-nih-yeh; withdraw cash)

✔ **kvitantsiya** (kvee-*tahn*-tsih-yuh; receipt)

✔ **zabyeritye kartu** (zuh-bee-*ree*-tee *kahr*-too; remove the card)

Spending money

Before you run out and spend your money, you may find it helpful to know the verb **platit'** (pluh-*teet';* to pay). Its conjugation appears in Table 3-1.

Table 3-1	Conjugation of *Platit'*	
Conjugation	*Pronunciation*	*Translation*
ya plachu	ya pluh-*choo*	I pay or I am paying
ty platish'	tih *plah*-teesh'	You pay or you are paying (informal singular)
on/ona/ ono platit	ohn/ah-*nah*/ ah-*noh plah*-teet	He/she/it pays or he/she/it is paying
my platim	mih *plah*-teem	We pay or we are paying
vy platitye	vih *plah*-tee-t'eh	You pay or you are paying (formal singular and plural)
oni platyat	ah-*nee plah*-t'uht	They pay or they are paying

Paying with credit cards

Although **kryeditnyye kartochki** (kree-*deet*-nih-eh *kahr*-tuhch-kee; credit cards) and **bankovskiye kartochki** (*bahn*-kuhf-skee-eh *kahr*-tuhch-kee; debit cards) have long been established in cities like Moscow and St. Petersburg, in other cities your attempts to pay with a credit card may not be as welcome. When making plans to pay with a credit card, it's worth asking

- ✔ **U vas mozhno zaplatit' kryeditnoj kartochkoj?** (oo vahs *mohzh*-nuh zuh-pluh-*teet'* kree-*deet*-nuhy *kahr*-tuhch-kuhy?; Do you accept credit cards?)

- ✔ **Ya mogu zaplatit' kryeditnoj kartochkoj?** (ya mah-*goo* zuh-pluh-*teet'* kree-*deet*-nuhy *kahr*-tuhch-kuhy?; Can I pay with a credit card?)

Some places, such as travel agencies, may charge you a fee when accepting payment by credit card. To find out where this is the case, you may want to ask **Vy vzymayetye komissionnyj sbor za oplatu kryeditnoj kartochkoj?** (vih vzih-*mah*-eh-t'eh kuh-mee-see-*oh*-nihy zbohr zuh ahp-*lah*-too kree-*deet*-nuhy *kahr*-tuhch-kuhy?; Do you charge a fee for paying with a credit card?)

Chapter 4

Making New Friends and Enjoying Small Talk

● ●

In This Chapter

▶ Using informal and formal versions of *you*

▶ Knowing phrases for *hello* and *goodbye*

▶ Introducing yourself and others

▶ Chatting about your life

● ●

Greetings and introductions in Russian are a bit more formal than in English. If you greet somebody correctly in Russian, that person is impressed and probably wants to get to know you better. If, however, you botch your greeting, you may get a funny look or even offend the person you're addressing.

In this chapter, we give you details on how to make your best first impression and then make small talk with your new friends.

To Whom Am 1 Speaking? Being Informal or Formal

When you want to say "hello" in Russian, it's important to know who you're talking to first. Unlike in English (but similar to French, German, or Spanish, for example), Russian uses two different words for the word *you* — informal **ty** (tih) and formal **vy** (vih).

Here's how to know when to use which form of *you:*

- In Russian, you're allowed to use the informal **ty** *only* when you're speaking to your parents, grandparents, siblings, children, and close friends.

- The formal **vy** is used in more formal situations when you talk to your boss, acquaintances, older people, or people you don't know very well, and any time you're speaking to more than one person.

As you get to know somebody better, you may switch to the informal **ty.** You even have a way of asking a person whether he or she is ready to switch to **ty: Mozhno na ty?** (*Mozh*-nuh nah tih?; May I call you informal *you?*) If the answer is **da!** (dah; yes), then you're free to start calling the person **ty.** If, however, the answer is **nyet!** (n'eht; no), you'd better wait until the person feels more comfortable with you!

Comings and Goings: Saying Hello and Goodbye

Greetings and goodbyes are essential Russian phrases to know — because they're the start and finish of every conversation.

Saying hello to different people

To greet one person with whom you're on informal **ty** (tih) terms, use the word **zdravstvuj** (*zdrah*-stvooy; hello). To greet a person with whom you're on formal **vy** (vih) terms or to address more than one person, use the longer word, **zdravstvujtye** (*zdrah*-stvooy-t'eh; hello). Note that the first letter *v* in **zdravstvujtye** is silent. Otherwise, it would be hard even for Russians to pronounce!

The informal way of saying "hello" in Russian is **privyet**! (pree-*v'eht*). It's similar to the English *hi*, and you should be on pretty familiar terms with a person before you use this greeting.

Here are some other ways to greet people, depending on what time of day it is:

✔ **Dobroye utro!** (*dohb*-ruh-eh *oo*-truh!;Good morning!): This is the greeting you use in the morning — until noon.

✔ **Dobryj dyen'!** (*dohb*-rihy d'ehn'!; Good afternoon!): This is the greeting you can use most of the day, except for early in the morning or late at night.

✔ **Dobryj vyechyer!** (*dohb*–rihy *v'eh*-ch'ehr! Good evening!): This is the greeting you would most likely use in the evening.

Handling "How are you?"

Here are the easiest and most popular ways to ask "How are you?":

✔ **Kak dyela?** (kahk dee-*lah*?): You use this phrase in rather informal settings.

✔ **Kak vy pozhivayetye?** (kahk vih puh-zhih-*vah*-eh-t'eh?): You use this phrase when speaking with your boss or somebody you've just met.

Here are some way to reply to **Kak dyela?**:

✔ **Khorosho** (khuh-rah-*shoh;* good)

✔ **Normal'no** (nahr-*mahl'*-nuh; normal or okay)

✔ **Nichyego** (nee-chee-*voh;* so-so [*literally:* nothing])

✔ **Nyeplokho** (nee-*ploh*-khuh; not bad)

✔ **Pryekrasno!** (pree-*krahs*-nuh!; wonderful)

✔ **Vyelikolyepno!** (vee-lee-kah-*l'ehp*-nuh!; terrific)

Although optimistic Americans don't hesitate to say "terrific" or "wonderful," Russians are usually more reserved. To be on the safe side, just say either **Nichyego** or **Nyeplokho.**

But don't stop there! Be sure to ask the person how she's doing. You simply say **A u vas?** (ah oo vahs?; And you? [formal]) If you want to be less formal, you say **A u tyebya?** (ah oo tee-*b'ah?;* And you?)

Taking your leave

The usual way to say "goodbye" in almost any situation is **Do svidaniya!** (duh svee-*dah*-nee-uh!), which literally means "'Til (the next) meeting." If you're on informal terms with somebody, you may also say **Poka** (pah-*kah;* bye or see you later).

The phrase you use while leave-taking in the evening or just before bed is **Spokojnoj nochi** (spah-*kohy*-nuhy *noh*-chee; Good night). The phrase works both for formal and informal situations.

Break the Ice: Making Introductions

Making a good first impression is important for the beginning of any relationship. This section shows you phrases to use when getting acquainted with someone, how to ask for somebody's name, and the best way to introduce your friends to new people.

Getting acquainted

In English, introducing yourself is the best way to start a conversation with somebody you don't know. Not so in Russian. Russians like to begin with first suggesting to get acquainted. They have two ways to say this:

✔ **Davajtye poznakomimsya!** (duh-*vahy*-t'eh puhz-nuh- *koh*-meem-suh!; Let's get acquainted!), when addressing a person formally or two or more people

✔ **Davaj poznakomimsya!** (duh-*vahy* puhz-nuh- *koh*-meem-suh!; Let's get acquainted!), when addressing a person informally

If somebody says one of these phrases to you, you should politely accept the suggestion by saying:

✔ **Davajtye!** (duh-vahy-t'eh!; Okay! [*literally:* Let's!]), when addressing a person formally or two or more people

✔ **Davaj!** (duh-vahy!; Okay! [*literally:* Let's!]), when addressing a person informally

Asking for people's names and introducing yourself

The formal version of "What is your name?" is **Kak vas zovut?** (kahk vahz zah-*voot?; literally:* What do they call you?). The informal version of "What is your name?" is **Kak tyebya zovut?** (kahk tee-*b'ah* zah-*voot?; literally:* What do they call you?). To introduce yourself in Russian, just say **Myenya zovut** (Mee-*n'ah* zah-*voot*) + your name.

After you're introduced to someone, you may want to say, "Nice to meet you." In Russian you say **ochyen' priyatno** (*oh*-cheen' pree-*yat*-nuh; *literally:* very pleasant). The person you've been introduced to may then reply **mnye tozhye** (mnye *toh*-zheh; same here). You use the phrases **ochyen' priyatno** and **mnye tozhye** in both formal and informal situations.

Saying names in Russian is a bit more complicated than in English because Russians use the *patronymic* (father's name) right after the first name. The patronymic usually has the ending **–vich** (veech), meaning "son of,"

or **–ovna** (*ohv*-nuh), meaning "daughter of." For example, a man named Boris, whose father's name is Ivan, would be known as Boris Ivanovich (Ivanovich is the patronymic). A woman named Anna whose father's name is Ivan would be known as Anna Ivanovna (Ivanovna is the patronymic). A Russian almost never formally addresses a person named Mikhail as just "Mikhail" but rather as "Mikhail" plus his patronymic with the suffix **–vich** (for instance, "Mikhail Nikolayevich" or "Mikhail Borisovich").

Men's last names and women's last names have different endings. That's because Russian last names have genders. Although most Russian male last names have the ending **–ov** (of), female names take the ending **–ova** (*ohv*-nuh). Imagine that your new acquaintance, Anna Ivanova, is a married woman. Her husband's last name isn't **Ivanova** (ee-vuh-*noh*-vuh), but **Ivanov** (ee-vuh-*nof*).

Introducing your friends and family

Everyday, common introductions are easy in Russian. When you want to introduce your friends, all you need to say is **Eto . . .** (eh-tuh . . . ; This is . . .). Then you simply add the name of the person.

To indicate that the person is an acquaintance or a colleague, you say one of two things:

- ✔ If the person is a man, you say **Eto moj znakomyj** (*eh*-tuh mohy znuh-*koh*-mihy; This is my acquaintance).

- ✔ If the person is a woman, you say **Eto moya znakomaya** (*eh*-tuh mah-*ya* znuh-*koh*-muh-yuh; This is my acquaintance).

Let Me Tell You Something: Talking about Yourself

What do people talk about when they first meet? The topics are highly predictable: You usually talk about yourself.

Stating where you're from

To start the conversation, you can say **Otkuda vy?** (aht-*koo*-duh vih?; Where are you from?). To answer, you can say:

- ✔ **Ya iz Amyeriki** (ya eez uh-*mye*-ree-kee; I am from America)

- ✔ **Ya zhivu v Amyerikye** (ya zhih-*voo* v uh-*meh*-ree-k'eh; I live in America)

After a Russian finds out your country of origin, he may ask you where in the country you're from (such as a city or a state). You may hear questions like

- ✔ **V kakom shtatye vy zhivyote?** (f kuh-*kohm* shtah-t'eh vih zhih-*vyo*-t'eh?; What state do you live in?)

- ✔ **Vy iz kakogo goroda?** (vih eez kuh-*koh*-vuh *goh*-ruh-duh?; What city are you from?)

You can answer:

- ✔ **Ya zhivu v Siyetlye** (ya zhih-*voo* f see-*yet*-l'eh; I live in Seattle)

- ✔ **Ya iz Siyetla** (ya ees see-*yet*-luh; I am from Seattle)

Notice that when the preposition **v** is followed by a noun beginning with an unvoiced consonant, it's pronounced like *f*, not *v*, and when the preposition **iz** is followed by a noun beginning with an unvoiced consonant, it's pronounced *ees*, not *eez*.

When you say **Ya zhivu v . . .** (ya zhih-voo v . . . ; I live in . . .), use the word describing the place where you live in the prepositional case, because the preposition **v** (in) takes that case. When saying **Ya iz . . .** (ya eez . . . ; I am from . . .), use the next word in the genitive case because the preposition **iz** (eez; from) requires genitive.

Telling your age

To inquire about someone's **vozrast** (vohz-ruhst; age) in Russian, you ask one of two questions:

- ✔ **Skol'ko tyebye lyet?** (*skohl'*-kuh tee-*b'eh* l'eht?; How old are you? [informal])

- ✔ **Skol'ko vam lyet?** (*skohl'*-kuh vahm l'eht; How old are you? [formal])

Answering isn't as simple as you may think. First of all, in Russia, age is seen as something that happens to you, something you can't control (and this is, after all, very true). That's why, instead of using the subject in the nominative case, Russian uses the dative form of the person whose age is being described. In Russian you say literally "To me is 23 years old."

The second tricky part of talking about your age is that the translation of the word *year(s)* depends on how old you are. This is how it works:

- ✔ If you're 1, 21, or 31 years old (in other words, if the numeral indicating your age is 1 or ends in 1), use the word **god** (goht; year), as in **Mnye dvadtsat' odin god** (mnye dvaht-tsuht' ah-deen goht; I am twenty-one years old).

- ✔ If the numeral denoting your age ends in a 2, 3, or 4, use the word **goda** (goh-duh; years), as in **Mnye dvadtsat' dva goda** (mnye *dvaht*-tsuht' dvah goh-duh; I am twenty-two years old).

✔ If the numeral denoting your age ends in 5, use the word **lyet,** as in **Mnye dvadlat' pyat' lyet** (mn'eh *dvaht*-tsuht' p'aht' l'eht; I am twenty-five years old).

✔ If the numeral denoting your age ends in a 6, 7, 8, or 9, or if your age is 10 through 20, use the word **lyet,** as in **Mnye dvadsat' syem' lyet** (mn'eh dvaht-tsuht' s'ehm' l'eht; I am twenty-seven years old).

Talking about Family

Family is a big part of Russian culture, so your Russian acquaintances will certainly be curious about yours.

Beginning with basic terms for family members

Your best bet is just to talk about the members of your family with your new Russian friend, using the following words:

✔ **mat'** (maht'; mother)

✔ **otyets** (ah-*t'ehts;* father)

✔ **rodityeli** (rah-*dee*-t'eh-lee; parents)

✔ **syn** (sihn; son)

✔ **synovya** (sih-nah-*v'ya;* sons)

✔ **doch'** (dohch'; daughter)

✔ **dochri** (*doh*-chee-ree; daughters)

✔ **zhyena** (zhih-*nah;* wife)

✔ **muzh** (moosh; husband)

✔ **brat** (braht; brother)

✔ **brat'ya** (*brah*-t'yuh; brothers)

✔ **syestra** (sees-*trah;* sister)

✔ **syostry** (*syos*-trih; sisters)

- **ryebyonok** (ree-*byo*-nuhk; child)
- **dyeti** (*d'eh*-tee, children)
- **babushka** (*bah*-boosh-kuh; grandmother)
- **dyedushka** (*d'eh*-doosh-kuh; grandfather)
- **babushka i dyedushka** (*bah*-boosh-kuh ee *d'eh*-doosh-kuh; grandparents [*literally:* grandmother and grandfather])
- **vnuk** (vnook; grandson)
- **vnuki** (*vnoo*-kee; grandsons)
- **vnuchka** (*vnooch*-kuh; granddaughter)
- **vnuchki** (*vnooch*-kee; granddaughters)
- **vnuki** (*vnoo*-kee; grandchildren)
- **dyadya** (*dya*-d'uh; uncle)
- **tyotya** (*tyo*-t'uh; aunt)
- **kuzyen** (koo-*zehn*; male cousin)
- **kuzina** (koo-*zee*-nuh; female cousin)
- **plyemyannik** (plee-*m'ah*-neek; nephew)
- **plyemyannitsa** (plee-*m'ah*-nee-tsuh; niece)
- **syem'ya** (seem'-*ya;* family)

Talking about family members with the verb "to have"

When talking about your family, use phrases like "I have a brother" and "I have a big family" and "I don't have any brothers or sisters." To say these phrases, you need to know how to use the verb **yest'** (yest'; to have).

Use the construction **U myenya yest'** . . . (oo mee-nya yest' . . . ; I have . . .) when talking about your own family:

- **U myenya yest' brat** (oo mee-*n'ah* yest' braht; I have a brother)

- **U myenya yest' syestra** (oo mee-*n'ah* yest' sees-*trah;* I have a sister)

If you want to say that you don't have a brother, a sister, a nephew, and so on, you use the construction **U myenya nyet** (oo mee-*n'ah* n'eht) plus a noun in the genitive case:

✔ **U myenya nyet brata** (oo mee-*n'ah* n'eht braht-uh; I don't have a brother)

✔ **U myenya nyet syestry** (oo mee-*n'ah* n'eht sees-*trih;* I don't have a sister)

The genitive plural forms of some family members are irregular, and you need to memorize them:

✔ **brat'yev** (*braht'*-yehf; brothers)

✔ **syestyor** (sees-*tyor;* sisters)

✔ **synovyej** (sih-nah-*v'ehy;* sons)

✔ **dochyeryej** (duh-chee-*r'ehy;* daughters)

✔ **dyetyej** (dee-*t'ehy;* children)

Where Do You Work?

Because what you do for living is crucial for a Russian's understanding of who you are, be prepared to answer the question **Kto vy po profyessii?** (ktoh vih puh-prah-*f'eh*-see-ee?; What do you do for living? [*literally:* What's your job?])

To answer the question about your profession, you just need the phrase **Ya** + your profession, as in **Ya yurist** (ya yoo-*reest;* I am a lawyer) or **Ya pryepodavatyel'** (ya pree-puh-duh-*vah*-t'ehl'; I am a professor). Here's a list of the most common professions:

✔ **agyent po nyedvizhimosti** (uh-*g'ehnt* puh need-*vee*-zhih-muhs-tee; real-estate agent)

✔ **aktrisa** (ahk-*tree*-suh; actress)

✔ **aktyor** (ahk-*tyor;* male actor)

✔ **archityektor** (uhr-khee-*t'ehk*-tuhr; architect)

- **bibliotyekar'** (beeb-lee-ah-*t'eh* huht ; librarian)
- **biznyesmyen** (beez-nehs-*m'ehn;* businessman)
- **bukhgaltyer** (bookh-*gahl*-t'ehr; accountant)
- **domokhozyajka** (duh-muh-khah-*zyahy*-kuh; homemaker)
- **inzhyenyer** (een-zhee-*n'ehr;* engineer)
- **khudozhnik** (khoo-*dohzh*-neek; artist, painter)
- **muzykant** (moo-zih-*kahnt;* musician)
- **myedbrat** (meed-*braht;* male nurse)
- **myedsyestra** (meed-sees-*trah;* female nurse)
- **myenyedzhyer** (*meh*-nehd-zhehr; manager)
- **pisatyel'** (pee-*sah*-t'ehl'; author, writer)
- **predprinimatyel** (preht-pree-nee-*mah*-t'ehl; a businessman or a businesswoman)
- **programmist** (pruh-gruh-*meest;* programmer)
- **pryepodavatyel'** (pree-puh-duh-*vah*-t'ehl'; professor at the university)
- **studyent** (stoo-*d'ehnt;* male student)
- **studyentka** (stoo-*d'ehnt*-kuh; female student)
- **uchityel'** (oo-*chee*-t'ehl'; male teacher)
- **uchityel'nitsa** (oo-*chee*-t'ehl'-nee-tsuh; female teacher)
- **vospitatyel'** (vuhs-pee-*tah*-t'ehl'; preschool teacher)
- **vrach** (vrahch; physician)
- **yurist** (yu-*reest;* attorney, lawyer)
- **zhurnalist** (zhoor-nuh-*leest;* journalist)
- **zunbnoj vrach** (zoob-*noy* vrahch; dentist)

You can also specify where you work. Russian doesn't have an equivalent for the English "I work for United" or "He works for FedEx." Instead of *for*, Russian uses its equivalent of *at* — prepositions **v** or **na.** Instead of saying, "I work for United," a Russian says, "I work at United."

The Russian prepositions **v** and **na** (at) require that the noun denoting a place should take the prepositional case. Here are some of the most common places people work. Say **Ya rabotayu . . .** (ya rah-*boh*-tuh-yu . . . ; I work . . .) plus one of these phrases:

✔ **doma** (*doh*-muh; from home)

✔ **na fabrikye** (nuh *fah*-bree-k'eh; at a light-industry factory)

✔ **na zavodye** (nuh zah-*voh*-d'eh; at a heavy-industry plant)

✔ **v bankye** (v *bahn*-k'eh; at a bank)

✔ **v bibliotyekye** (v beeb-lee-ah-*t'eh*-k'eh; in a library)

✔ **v bol'nitsye** (v bahl'-*nee*-tseh; at a hospital)

✔ **v byuro nyedvizhimosti** (v b'u-*roh* need-*vee*-zhih-muhs-tee; at a real-estate agency)

✔ **v kommyerchyeskoj firmye** (f kah-*m'ehr*-chees-kuhy *feer*-m'eh; at a business firm, company)

✔ **v laboratorii** (v luh-buh-ruh-*toh*-ree-ee; in a laboratory)

✔ **v magazinye** (v muh-guh-*zee*-n'eh; at a store)

✔ **v shkolye** (f *shkoh*-l'eh; at a school)

✔ **v uchryezhdyenii** (v ooch-reezh-*d'eh*-nee-ee; at an office)

✔ **v univyersityetye** (v oo-nee-veer-see-*t'eh*-t'eh; at a university)

✔ **v yuridichyeskoj** firmye (v yu-ree-*dee*-chees-kuhy *feer*-m'eh; at a law firm)

Let's Get Together: Giving and Receiving Contact Information

Just before you're about to take your leave from a new Russian acquaintance, you probably want to exchange contact information. The easiest way to do this is just hand over your business card and say **Eto moya vizitnaya kartochka** (*eh*-tuh mah-yah vee-*zeet*-nah-yuh *kahr*-tuhch-kuh; This is my card [literally: this is my visiting card]). In case you don't have a business card, you need to know these phrases:

- **Moj adryes . . .** (mohy *ah*-dr'ehs . . . ; My address is . . .)
- **Moya ulitsa . . .** (mah-*ya* oo-lee-tsuh . . . ; My street is . . .)
- **Moj nomyer doma . . .** (mohy *noh*-m'ehr *doh*-muh . . . ; My house number is . . .)
- **Moj indyeks . . .** (mohy *een*-dehks . . . ; My zip code is . . .)
- **Moj nomyer tyelyefona** (moy *noh*-mer tee-lee-*foh*-nuh . . . ; My telephone number is . . .)

After you give your contact info, be sure to get your new friend's address, phone number, and e-mail address. You can use these phrases:

- **Kakoj u vas nomyer tyelyefona?** (kuh-*kohy* oo vahs *noh*-meer tee-lee-*foh*-nuh?; What's your phone number?)
- **Kakoj u vas adryes?** (kuh-*kohy* oo vahs *ahd*-r'ehs?; What's your address?)
- **Kakoj u vas adryes elektronnoj pochty?** (kuh-*kohy* oo vahs *ahd*-r'ehs eh-l'ehk-*troh*-nuhy *pohch*-tih?; What's your e-mail address?)

I'm Sorry! I Don't Understand

When you first start conversing in Russian, there will probably be a lot you don't understand. You can signal that you don't understand something in several ways. Choose the phrase you like best, or use them all to really get the message across:

- ✔ **Izvinitye, ya nye ponyal.** (eez-vee-*nee*-t'eh ya nee *pohh*-n'uhl; Sorry, I didn't understand. [masculine])

- ✔ **Izvinitye, ya nye ponyala.** (eez-vee-*nee*-t'eh ya nee puh-nee-*lah;* Sorry, I didn't understand. [feminine])

- ✔ **Izvinitye, ya plokho ponimayu po-russki.** (eez-vee-*nee*-t'eh ya *ploh*-khuh puh-nee-*mah*-yu pah-*roos*-kee; Sorry, I don't understand Russian very well.)

- ✔ **Govoritye, pozhalujsta, myedlyennyeye!** (guh-vah-*ree*-t'eh pah-*zhahl*-stuh *m'ehd*-lee-nee-eh!; Speak more slowly, please!)

- ✔ **Kak vy skazali?** (kahk vih skuh-*zah*-lee?; What did you say?)

- ✔ **Povtoritye, pozhalujsta.** (puhf-tah-ree-t'eh pah-*zhah*-luh-stuh; Could you please repeat that?)

- ✔ **Vy govoritye po-anglijski?** (vih guh-vah-*ree*-t'eh puh uhn-*gleey*-skee?; Do you speak English?)

Chapter 5

Enjoying a Drink and a Snack (or a Meal!)

. . . .

In This Chapter

▶ Talking about food fundamentals

▶ Eating breakfast, lunch, and dinner

▶ Shopping for food

▶ Dining in restaurants and cafes

. . . .

Russians are famous for their bountiful cuisine. Whether you like homemade food or prefer to go out to Russian restaurants, knowing how to talk about food is helpful.

Focusing on Food Basics

Russian has a rich variety of words and expressions related to eating and drinking. In this section, we tell you how to say you're thirsty and hungry in Russian, tell you how to talk about the different eating utensils, and give you an overview of basic Russian table etiquette.

Eating up

When Russians are hungry they don't say "I'm hungry." Instead they say **Ya khochu yest'** (ya khah-*choo* yest'; I'm hungry [*literally*: I want to eat). If you want to ask somebody if he or she is hungry, you say.

✔ **Ty khochyesh' yest'?** (tih *khoh*-chehsh' yest'?; Are you hungry? [*literally:* Do you want to eat?], informal)

✔ **Vy khotitye yest'?** (vih khah-*tee*-t'eh yest'?; Are you hungry? [*literally:* Do you want to eat?], formal and plural)

In addition to these expressions, you may also hear one of the following phrases:

✔ **Vy golodnyj?** (vih gah-*lohd*-nihy?; Are you hungry?), when speaking to a male

✔ **Vy golodnaya?** (vih gah-*lohd*-nuh-yuh?; Are you hungry?), when speaking to a female

✔ **Vy golodnyye?** (vih gah-*lohd*-nih-eh; Are you hungry?), when speaking to multiple people

To answer these questions, you say:

✔ **Ya golodnyj** (ya gah-*lohd*-nihy; I'm hungry), if you're male

✔ **Ya golodnaya** (ya gah-*lohd*-nuh-'uh; I'm hungry), if you're female

Note that these phrases, however, have a particular flavor. In Russia **golod** (*goh*-luht; hunger) is a word that carries tragic historical connotations. So although it's perfectly acceptable to use the preceding expressions, you should know that they also carry this darker, secondary meaning.

Table 5-1 shows you how to conjugate the Russian verb **yest'** (yest'; to eat) for all the different pronouns. It's an irregular verb, so you just have to memorize it.

Table 5-1	Conjugation of Yest'	
Conjugation	Pronunciation	Translation
ya yem	ya yem	I eat or I am eating
ty yesh'	tih yesh'	You eat or you are eating (informal singular)
on/ona/ ono yest	ohn/ah-*nah*/ ah-*noh* yest	He/she/it eats or he/she/it is eating
my yedim	mih yee-*deem*	We eat or we are eating
vy yeditye	vih yee-*dee*-t'eh	You eat or you are eating (formal singular and plural)
oni yedyat	ah-*nee*-yee-*dyat*	They eat or they are eating

Drinking up

If you feel thirsty, you say **Ya khochu pit'** (ya khah-*choo* peet'; I'm thirsty [*literally:* I want to drink]). When you want to ask somebody whether he or she is thirsty, you say **Ty khochyesh' pit'?** (tih *khoh*-chehsh' peet'?; Are you thirsty? [*literally:* Do you want to drink?], informal) or **Vy khotitye pit'?** (vih khah-tee-t'eh peet'?; Are you thirsty? [*literally:* Do you want to drink?], formal).

The drinking verb **pit'** (peet'; to drink) has an unruly conjugation, as shown in Table 5-2.

Table 5-2	Conjugation of Pit'	
Conjugation	Pronunciation	Translation
ya p'yu	ya p'yu	I drink or I am drinking
ty p'yosh'	tih p'yosh'	You drink or you are drinking (informal singular)

(continued)

Table 5-2 *(continued)*

Conjugation	Pronunciation	Translation
on/ona/ ono p'yot	ohn/ah-*nah*/ ah-*noh* p'yot	He/she/it drinks or he/she/it is drinking
my p'yom	mih p'yom	We drink or we are drinking
vy p'yotye	vih p'yo-t'eh	You drink or you are drinking (formal singular and plural)
oni p'yut	ah-nee p'yut	They drink or they are drinking

Just as in English, the Russian statement **On/ona p'yot** (ohn/ah-*nah* p'yot; He/she drinks) in certain contexts can signify that the person is an alcoholic. If that's not your intention, you may want to add a direct object to the sentence to clarify your meaning.

Some common **napitki** (nuh-*peet*-kee; beverages) you may use as the direct objects are

- ✔ **sok** (sohk; juice)
- ✔ **chaj** (chahy; tea)
- ✔ **kofye** (*koh*-f'eh; coffee)
- ✔ **vodka** (*voht*-kuh; vodka)
- ✔ **pivo** (*pee*-vuh; beer)
- ✔ **vino** (vee-*noh;* wine)
- ✔ **kvas** (kvahs; a nonalcoholic beverage made of bread)

To say "I drink coffee" in Russian, you say **Ya p'yu kofye** (yah p'yu *koh*-f'eh). "I'm drinking vodka" is **Ya p'yu vodku** (yah p'yu *voht'*-koo). Notice that, in this sentence, **vodka** become **vodku,** the accusative-case form of the noun, because it's the direct object of the sentence.

Using utensils and tableware

Here's a list of the most common eating utensils and tableware:

- ✔ **blyudyechko** (*bl'u*-deech-kuh; tea plate)
- ✔ **chashka** (*chahsh*-kuh; cup)
- ✔ **chaynaya lozhka** or **lozhyechka** (*chahy*-nuh-'uh *lohsh*-kuh or *loh*-zhihch-kuh; teaspoon)
- ✔ **glubokaya taryelka** (gloo-*boh*-kuh-'uh tuh-*r'ehl*-kuh; soup bowl)
- ✔ **kruzhka** (*kroosh*-kuh; mug)
- ✔ **lozhka** (*lohsh*-kuh; spoon)
- ✔ **nozh** (nohsh; knife)
- ✔ **salfyetka** (sahl-*f'eht*-kuh; napkin)
- ✔ **stakan** (stuh-*kahn*; glass)
- ✔ **taryelka** (tah-*r'ehl*-kuh; plate)
- ✔ **vilka** (*veel*-kuh; fork)

If you need to borrow a spoon from someone, you may ask that person by saying **Mozhno lozhku?** (*mohzh*-nuh *lohsh*-koo; Can I have a spoon?).

Making room for the Russian tea tradition

The famous Russian tradition called **chayepitiye** (chee-*pee*-tee-eh) is derived of two words — **chaj** (chahy; tea) and the noun **pitiye** (*pee*-tee-eh; drinking). Russians love tea almost as much as Brits do and drink it in huge quantities, usually in big glasses. In the old days, they used a **samovar** (suh-mah-*vahr*) — a special, huge tea-kettle, placed in the middle of the table. Russians usually drink tea with **sakhar** (*sah*-khuhr; sugar) and home-made berry preserves called **varayen'ye** (vah-*r'ehn*-ye).

The construction **Mozhno . . .** (*mozh*-nuh; Can/May I have . . .) + a noun is quite common in Russian. The noun takes the accusative case.

Enjoying Different Meals

Russians eat three meals a day: **zavtrak** (*zahf*-truhk; breakfast), **obyed** (ah-*b'eht;* dinner), and **uzhin** (*oo*-zhihn; supper). But Russian meals have quite a few peculiarities, which we tell you about in the following sections.

Russian for "to cook" is **gotovit'** (gah-*toh*-veet'). So, if cooking is one of your hobbies, you can now proudly say **Ya lyublyu gotovit'** (ya lyub-*lyu* gah-*toh*-veet'; I like/love to cook) when asked **Vy lyubitye gotovit'?** (vih *lyu*-bee-t'eh gah-*toh*-veet'; Do you like to cook?)

What's for breakfast? Almost anything!

The Russian breakfast is called **zavtrak** (*zahf*-truhk). What can you eat for **zavtrak?** The real question is what *can't* you eat! In contrast to American cereal, fruit, or bagels, or the British porridge, or the French croissant and jam, the Russian **zavtrak** is very flexible. Some Russian breakfast favorites include

- **butyerbrod s kolbasoj** (boo-tehr-*broht* s kuhl-buh-sohy; sausage sandwich)

- **butyerbrod s syrom** (boo-tehr-*broht* s *sih*-ruhm; cheese sandwich)

- **kasha** (*kah*-shuh; cooked grain served hot with milk, sugar, and butter)

- **kofye s molokom** (*koh*-f'eh s muh-lah-*kohm;* coffee with milk)

- **kolbasa** (kuhl-buh-*sah;* sausage)
- **ryofk** (kee-*feer;* kefir)
- **syelyodka s kartoshkoj** (see-*lyot*-kuh s kahr-*tohsh*-kuhy; herring with potatoes)
- **varyen'ye** (vuh-*r'ehn'*-yeh; jam)
- **yaichnitsa** (ee-*eesh*-nee-tsuh; fried or scrambled eggs)

If you're not quite ready for **syelyodka s kartoshkoj** in the morning, use the following words to order Western-style breakfast foods:

- **behkon** (bee-*kohn;* bacon)
- **bliny** (blee-*nih;* pancakes)
- **kasha** (*kah*-shuh; cereal)
- **kukuruznyye khlop'ya** (koo-koo-*rooz*-nih-eh *khlohp'*yuh; corn flakes)
- **moloko** (muh-lah-*koh;* milk)
- **ovsyanka** (ahf-*s'ahn*-kuh; oatmeal)
- **sok** (sohk; juice)
- **tost** (tohst; toast)
- **yajtsa** (*yay*-tsuh; boiled eggs)
- **yaichnitsa** (ee-*eesh*-nee-tsuh; fried/scrambled eggs)

Let's do dinner (not lunch)

Obyed (ah-*b'eht;* dinner) is the main meal of the day and it's usually eaten as a midday meal between 1 p.m. and 3 p.m. For their midday meal, Russians enjoy a four-course meal consisting of **zakuski** (zuh-*koos*-kee; appetizers), **sup** (soop; soup), **vtoroye** (ftah-*roh*-yeh; the second or main course), and **dyesyert** (dee-*s'ehrt;* dessert), also called **tryet'ye** (*tr'eh*-t'ye; third course).

The most popular Russian **zakuski** are

- **baklazhannaya ikra** (buh-klah-_zhun_-nuh-yuh eek-_rah;_ eggplant caviar)

- **kapustnyj salat** (kah-_poost_-nihy suh-_laht;_ cabbage salad)

- **salat iz ogurtsov i pomidorov** (suh-_laht_ iz ah-goor-_tsohf_ ee puh-mee-_doh_-ruhf; salad made of tomatoes and cucumbers)

- **salat olivye** (suh-_laht_ uh-lee-_v'ye;_ meat salad)

- **studyen'** (_stoo_-deen'; beef in aspic)

- **syelyodka** (see-_lyot_-kuh; herring)

- **vinyegryet** (vee-nee-_gr'eht;_ mixed vegetable salad made with beets, carrots, and pickle)

- **vyetchina s goroshkom** (veet-chee-_nah_ s gah-_rohsh_-kuhm; ham with peas)

After **zakuski** comes the **sup.** You have many different kinds to choose from:

- **borsh'** (bohrsh'; beet root soup)

- **bul'yon** (bool'-_yon;_ broth)

- **kurinyj sup** (koo-ree-nihy soop; chicken soup)

- **molochnyj sup** (mah-_lohch_-nihy soop; milk soup)

- **sh'i** (sh'ee; cabbage soup)

- **ukha** (oo-_khah;_ fish soup)

After the **sup** comes the main course, usually called **vtoroye** (ftah-_roh_-eh; _literally:_ second course). Here are some typical Russian favorites:

- **bifshtyeks** (beef-_shtehks;_ beefsteak)

- **bifstroganov** (behf-_stroh_-guh-nuhf; beef stroganoff)

- **gamburgyer** (gahm-_boor_-geer; hamburger) (Russians are still getting used to this one, but

they do prefer **kotlyety** to **gamburgyery;** old
habits die hard.)

✔ **golubtsy** (guh-loop-*tsih;* stuffed cabbage rolls)

✔ **griby** (gree-*bih;* mushrooms)

✔ **kotlyety** (kaht-*l'eh*-tih; ground meat patties)

✔ **kotlyety s kartoshkoj** (kaht-*l'eh*-tih s kuhr-*tohsh*-
kuhy; meat patty with potatoes)

✔ **kuritsa** (*koo*-ree-tsuh; chicken)

✔ **makarony** (muh-kuh-*roh*-nih; pasta)

✔ **pitsa** (*pee*-tsuh; pizza) (This one is a relative
novelty in Russian cuisine.)

✔ **pyechyen'** (*p'eh*-cheen'; liver)

✔ **ryba** (*rih*-buh; fish)

✔ **schnitzyel'** (*shnee*-tsehl'; schnitzel)

✔ **sosiski** (sah-*sees*-kee; frankfurters)

✔ **zharkoye** (zhuhr-*koh*-ee; any meat cooked in
an oven)

The main course is usually served with **kartoshka**
(kuhr-*tohsh*-kuh; potatoes), **makarony** (muh-kuh-*roh*-
nih; pasta), and **ris** (rees; rice), and it's always served
with **khlyeb** (khlep; bread).

After the main course comes **dyesyert** (dee-*s'ehrt;*
dessert), or **tryet'ye** (*tr'eh*-t'ye; third course).
This course usually consists of some kind of

✔ **kompot** (kahm-poht; compote)

✔ **kisyel'** (kee-*s'ehl';* drink made of fruit and starch)

✔ **morozhenoye** (mah-*roh*-zhih-nuh-eh; ice cream)

✔ **pyechyen'ye** (pee-*chehn'*-eh; cookies)

✔ **pirog** (pee-*rohk;* pie)

✔ **tort** (tohrt; cake)

Some typical beverages that Russians drink in the middle of the day are **sok** (sohk; juice) **chaj** (chahy, tea) **kofje** (koh-f'eh, coffee), and **voda** (vah-*dah;* water), although the latter doesn't enjoy as much popularity as it does in the United States, for example.

A simple supper

The last meal of the day is called **uzhin** (*oo*-zhihn; supper), and it's usually eaten with the family around the kitchen or dining room table. Just as with **obyed** (dinner), soup and a main course are often served for **uzhin.** **Butyerbrody** (boo-tehr-*broh*-dih; open-sided sandwiches) may also be served, and several cups of **chaj** (chahy; tea) often conclude the evening meal. Some other Russian supper favorites include

- ✓ **blinchiki** (*bleen*-chee-kee; crepes)

- ✓ **pyel'myeni** (peel'-*m'eh*-nee; Russian ravioli)

- ✓ **syrniki** (*sihr*-nee-kee; patties made of cottage cheese)

- ✓ **tvorog so smyetanoj** (*tvoh*-ruhk suh smee-*tah*-nuhy; cottage cheese with sour cream)

Going Out for Groceries

If you want to make a quick trip to the **produktovyyj magazin** (pruh-dook-*toh*-vihy muh-guh-*zeen;* grocery store) or spend a leisurely day at the Russian **rynok** (*rih*-nuhk; market), you have to know how to buy food products in Russian.

Picking out produce

Buying produce at a farmers' market is very common. Russians are convinced that produce is much fresher there than in regular grocery stores. Table 5-3 has a list of some of the more popular produce items you may want to buy:

Table 5-3	Produce	
Russian	*Pronunciation*	*Translation*
arbuzy	uhr-*boo*-zih	Watermelons
balkazhany	buhk-luh-*zhah*-nih	Eggplants
chyernika	cheer-*nee*-kuh	Blueberries
chyesnok	chees-*nohk*	Garlic
gorokh	guh-*rohkh*	Peas
grushi	*groo*-shih	Pears
kapusta	kuh-*poos*-tuh	Cabbages
klubnika	kloob-*nee*-kuh	Strawberries
luk	look	Onions
malina	muh-*lee*-nuh	Raspberries
morkov'	mahr-*kohf'*	Carrots
ogurtsy	uh-goor-*tsih*	Cucumbers
pomidory	puh-mee-*doh*-rih	Tomatoes
pyeryets	*p'eh*-reets	Peppers
ryediska	ree-*dees*-kuh	Radishes
svyokla	*svyok*-luh	Beets
vinograd	vee-nah-*grahd*	Grapes
vishnya	*veesh*-n'uh	Cherries
yabloki	*ya*-bluh-kee	Apples

Surveying other grocery items

Chances are, most of the food items you want to buy can be found at the **rynok,** but you can also buy the food products you need at **produktovyye magaziny** (pruh-dook-*toh*-vih-ee muh-gah-*zee*-nih; grocery stores). We list some of the most common food items in Table 5-4.

Table 5-4	Common Food Items	
Russian	*Pronunciation*	*Translation*
baranina	buh-*rah*-nee-nuh	Mutton
bubliki	*boob*-lee-kee	Bagels
bulka	*bool*-kuh	White bread
chaj	chahy	Tea
chyornyj khleb	*chyor*-nihy khl'ehp	Dark bread
farsh	fahrsh	Ground meat
gorchitsa	gahr-*chee*-tsuh	Mustard
govyadina	gah-*vya*-dee-nuh	Beef
jogurt	*yo*-goort	Yogurt
khlyeb	khl'ehp	Bread
kofye	*koh*-f'eh	Coffee
kolbasa	kuhl-buh-*sah*	Sausage
kuritsa	*koo*-ree-tsuh	Chicken
kyefir	kee-*feer*	Kefir
majonyez	muh-ee-*nehs*	Mayonnaise
makarony	muh-kuh-*roh*-nih	Pasta

Russian	Pronunciation	Translation
maslo	*mahs*-luh	Butter
moloko	muh-lah-*koh*	Milk
muka	moo-*kah*	Flour
myaso	*mya*-suh	Meat
podsolnechnoye maslo	paht-*sohl*-neech-nuh-eh *mahs*-luh	Sunflower oil
pyeryets	*p'eh*-reets	Pepper
ris	rees	Rice
ryba	*rih*-buh	Fish
sakhar	*sah*-khuhr	Sugar
smyetana	smee-*tah*-nuh	Sour cream
sok	sohk	Juice
sol'	sohl'	Salt
svinina	svee-*nee*-nuh	Pork
syr	sihr	Cheese
voda	vah-*dah*	Water
vyetchina	veet-chee-*nah*	Ham
yajtsa	*yahy*-tsuh	Eggs

Eating Out with Ease

Eating out at Russian restaurants and cafes can be a lot of fun, especially if you know Russian. In the following sections, we go over the different kinds of restaurants you can go to, how to reserve your table, the right way to order a meal, and how to pay your bill.

Deciding on a place to eat

You can find lots of different places to eat out, Russian-style, depending on your mood and budget. If you're in the mood for a night of culinary delights, with a full eight-course meal, lots of drinks, and live music, check out a fancy Russian **ryestoran** (ree-stah-*rahn;* restaurant).

A more affordable everyday option is a **kafye** (kuh-*feh;* cafe), which can serve anything from coffee and ice cream, to pancakes, to pies. Cafes are usually privately owned and have such interesting names (often unrelated to food) that if you pass one of them on the street, you may not even recognize it as a place to eat! But if you follow that delicious smell under your nose, you may wind up at one of these delightful little places:

✔ **blinnaya** (*blee*-nuh-yuh; cafe that serves pancakes)

✔ **chyeburyechnya** (chee-boo-*r'ehch*-nuh-yuh; cafe that serves meat pies)

✔ **kafye-morozhenoye** (kuh-*feh* mah-*roh*-zhih-nuh-eh; ice-cream parlor)

✔ **pirozhkovya** (pee-rahsh-*koh*-vuh-yuh; cafe that serves small pies)

✔ **pyel'myennya** (*peel'*-m'ehn-nuh-yuh; place that serves Russian ravioli)

✔ **pyshyechnaya** (*pih*-shihch-nuh-yuh; donut shop)

✔ **stolovaya** (stah-*loh*-vuh-yuh; dining room)

✔ **zakusochnaya** (zuh-*koo*-suhch-nuh-yuh; snack bar)

After you decide which restaurant to go to, pick up the phone and make a reservation:

✓ If you're a man, say, **Ya khotyel by zakazat' stolik na syegodnya** (ya khah-*t'ehl* bih zuh-kuh-*zaht'* stoh-leek nuh see-*vohd*-n'uh, I'd like to reserve a table for tonight).

✓ If you're a woman, say, **Ya khotyela by zakazat' stolik na syegodnya** (ya khah-*tye*-luh bih zuh-kuh-*zaht'* stoh-leek nuh see-*vohd*-n'uh; I'd like to reserve a table for tonight).

The art of ordering a meal

After you arrive at the restaurant and are seated by the **myetrdotyel'** (mehtr-dah-*tehl;* maitre d'), the **ofitsiant** (uh-fee-tsih-*ahnt;* waiter) or **ofitsiantka** (uh-fee-tsih-*ahnt*-kuh; waitress) will bring you a **myenyu** (mee-*n'u;* menu). In a nice restaurant, all the dishes in the menu are usually listed in English as well as Russian.

When you open the menu, you'll notice it's divided into several subsections, which is how items are usually eaten and ordered in a Russian restaurant:

✓ **zakuski** (zuh-*koos*-kee; appetizers)

✓ **supy** (soo-*pih;* soups)

✓ **goryachiye blyuda** (gah-*rya*-chee-eh *bly'u*-duh; main dishes)

✓ **sladkiye blyuda** (*slaht*-kee-eh *bl'u*-duh; dessert)

✓ **alkogol'nye napitki** (ahl-kah-*gohl'*-nih-eh nuh-*peet*-kee; alcoholic drinks)

✓ **bezalkogol'niye napitki** (beez-uhl-kah-*gohl'*-nih-eh nuh-*peet*-kee; nonalcoholic beverages)

When the waiter asks you **Chto vy budyetye zakazy-vat'?** (shtoh vih *boo*-d'eh-t'eh zuh-*kah*-zih-vuht'?; What would you like to order?), just say **Ya budu** + the name of the item you're ordering in the accusative case. (For more on forming the accusative, see

Chapter 2.) For example, you may say something like: **Ya budu kotlyetu s kartofyelyem i salat iz nomidorov** (ya boo-doo kahht-*l eh*-tih s kahr-*toh*-fee-l'ehm ee suh-*laht* ees puh-mee-*doh*-ruhf; I'll have meat patty with potatoes and tomato salad).

The waiter may also ask you specifically **Chto vy budyetye pit'?** (shtoh vih *boo*-dee-t'eh peet'?; What would you like to drink?). To answer, you simply say **Ya budu** (ya *boo*-doo; I will have) + the name of the drink you want in the accusative case.

When you say **Ya budu** + the food or drink item, what you're really saying is **Ya budu yest' . . .** (ya *boo*-doo yest' . . . ; I will eat . . .) or **Ya budu pit' . . .** (ya *boo*-doo peet' . . . ; I will drink . . .). The verbs **yest'** (yest'; to eat) and **pit'** (peet'; to drink) force the noun coming after them into the accusative case because it's a direct object. When you order, you skip the verbs **yest'** and **pit'**, but they're implied.

Receiving and paying the bill

When it comes time to ask for the bill, don't expect the waiter to bring it automatically. When the waiter is in the vicinity, try to attract his attention by either waving or smiling to him or just saying (loudly, if necessary — Russians are very direct!) **Rasschitajtye nas pozhalujsta!** (ruh-shee-*tahy*-t'eh nahs pah-*zhahl*-stuh!; Check please!)

If the waiter returns before you ask him for the bill, he may tell you how much you owe by saying **S vas . . .** (s vahs; you owe [*literally:* from you is due . . .]). If your meal costs 200 rubles 41 kopecks, the waiter will say **S vas dvyesti rublyej sorok odna kopyejka** (s vahs *dv'ehs-tee*-roob-l'ehy soh-ruhk ahd-*nah* kah-*p'ehy*-kuh; You owe two hundred rubles and forty-one kopeks).

Chapter 6

Shop 'Til You Drop

. . . .

In This Chapter

▶ Finding out where to shop

▶ Looking for clothes

▶ Selecting the items you want

▶ Paying the bill

. . . .

*W*hether you're hardcore or just window shopping, this chapter gives you what you need to know.

Where and How to Buy Things the Russian Way

You can buy anything (other than food) in either a **univyermagi** (oo-nee-veer-*mah*-gee; department stores) or **magaziny** (muh-guh-*zee*-nih; stores). If you're looking for something specific, you'll want to check out some of the following stores:

- ✔ **antikvarnyj magazin** (uhn-tee-*kvahr*-nihy muh-guh-*zeen;* antique store)

- ✔ **aptyeka** (uhp-*tye*-kuh; pharmacy)

- ✔ **byel'yo** (beel'-*yo;* intimate apparel)

- ✔ **dyetskaya odyezhda** (*d'eht*-skuh-yuh ah-*d'ehzh*-duh; children's apparel)

- ✔ **elyektrotovary** (eh-*l'ehk*-truh-tah-*vah*-rih; electrical goods)

- ✔ **fototovary** (*foh*-tuh-tah-*vah*-rih; photography store)

- ✔ **galantyeryeya** (guh-luhn-tee-*r'eh*-yuh; haberdashery)

- ✔ **gazyetnyj kiosk** (guh-*z'eht*-nihy kee-*ohsk;* newsstand)

- ✔ **golovnyye ubory** (guh-lahv-*nih*-eh oo-*boh*-rih; hats)

- ✔ **kantsyelyarskiye tovary** (kuhn-tsih-*l'ahr*-skee-eh tah-*vah*-rih; stationery)

- ✔ **khozyajstvyennyj magazin** (khah-*z'ay*-stv'eh-nihy muh-guh-*zeen;* household goods, hardware store)

- ✔ **komissionnyj magazin** (kuh-mee-see-*ohn*-nihy muh-guh-*zeen;* secondhand store)

- ✔ **kosmyetika** (kahs-*m'eh*-tee-kuh; makeup)

- ✔ **muzhskaya odyezhda** (moosh-*skah*-yuh ah-*d'ehzh*-duh; men's apparel)

- ✔ **muzykal'nyye instrumyenty** (moo-zih-*kahl'*-nih-eh een-stroo-*myen*-tih; musical instruments)

- ✔ **odyezhda** (ah-*d'ehzh*-duh; clothing)

- ✔ **parfumyeriya** (puhr-fyu-*m'eh*-ree-yuh; perfumery)

- ✔ **posuda** (pah-*soo*-duh; tableware)

- ✔ **sportivnyye tovary** (spahr-*teev*-nih-eh tah-*vah*-rih; sporting goods)

- ✔ **suvyeniry** (soo-vee-*nee*-rih; souvenir store)

- ✔ **tkani** (*tkah*-nee; textiles)

- ✔ **tsvyety** (tsvee-*tih;* florist)

- ✔ **vyerkhnyaya odyezhda** (*vyerkh*-n'eh-yuh ah-*dyezh*-duh; outerwear)

- ✔ **yuvyelirnyj magazin** (yu-vee-*leer*-nihy muh-gah-*zeen;* jewelry store)

- ✔ **zhyenskaya odyezhda** (*zhehn*-skuh-yuh ah-*d'ehzh*-duh; women's apparel)

The easiest way to find out whether a Russian store is open is to go there and look for a sign hanging in the

door or window with one of these two words on it:
Otkryto (oht-*krih*-tuh; Open) or **Zakryto** (zuh-*krit*-tuh;
Closed). The next best way is just to call. Here are
some ways to ask about store hours:

> ✔ **Do kotorogo chasa otkryt magazin?** (duh kuh-
> *toh*-ruh-vuh *chah*-suh aht-*kriht* muh-guh-*zeen*;
> 'Til what time is the store open?)

> ✔ **V voskryesyen'ye magazin otrkryt?** (v vuhs-
> kree-*s'ehn'*-yeh muh-guh-*zeen* aht-*kriht*; Is the
> store open on Sunday?)

> ✔ **Kogda magazin zakryvayetsya?** (kahg-*dah* muh-
> guh-*zeen* zuh-krih-*vah*-eht-s'uh; When does the
> store close?)

> ✔ **Kogda zavtra otkryvayetsya magazin?**
> (kahg-*dah* zahf-truh uht-krih-*vah*-eht-s'uh
> muh-guh-*zeen*; When does the store open
> tomorrow?)

You Wear It Well: Shopping for Clothes

Russian folk wisdom has it that people's first
impression of you is based on the way you're
dressed. That's why you're likely to see
Russians well-dressed in public, even in
informal situations. To keep up, you'll want
the phrases in the following sections.

Seeking specific items of clothing

If you're looking for outerwear, you want to go to the
store or department called **vyerkhnyaya odyezhda**
(*v'ehrkh*-n'eh-yuh ah-*d'ehzh*-duh; outerwear). There
you'll find things like a

> ✔ **kurtka** (*koort*-kuh; short coat or warmer jacket)

> ✔ **pal'to** (puhl'-*toh;* coat)

> ✔ **plash'** (plahsh'; raincoat or trench coat)

If you need a new pair of shoes, drop in to the store or department called **obuv'** (*oh*-boof'; footwear) and choose among

- ✔ **bosonozhki** (buh-sah-*nohsh*-kee; women's sandals)
- ✔ **botinki** (bah-*teen*-kee; laced shoes)
- ✔ **krossovki** (krah-*sohf*-kee; sneakers)
- ✔ **sandalii** (suhn-*dah*-lee-ee; sandals)
- ✔ **sapogi** (suh-pah-*gee*; boots)
- ✔ **tufli** (*toof*-lee; lighter shoes for men and most shoes for women)

In the **galantyeryeya** (guh-luhn-tee-*r'eh*-yuh; haberdashery) you can buy all kinds of little things, both for her and for him, such as

- ✔ **chulki** (chool-*kee;* stockings)
- ✔ **chyemodan** (chee-mah-*dahn;* suitcase)
- ✔ **galstuk** (*gahl*-stook; necktie)
- ✔ **khalat** (khuh-*laht;* robe)
- ✔ **kolgotki** (kahl-*goht*-kee; pantyhose)
- ✔ **kupal'nik** (koo-*pahl'*-neek; bathing suit)
- ✔ **noski** (nahs-*kee;* socks)
- ✔ **nosovoj platok** (nuh-sah-*vohy* pluh-*tohk;* handkerchief)
- ✔ **ochki** (ahch-*kee;* eyeglasses)
- ✔ **pizhama** (pee-*zhah*-muh; pajamas)
- ✔ **pyerchatki** (peer-*chaht*-kee; gloves)
- ✔ **raschyoska** (ruh-*sh'yos*-kuh; hairbrush/comb)
- ✔ **ryemyen'** (ree-*myen';* belt)
- ✔ **sumka** (*soom*-kuh; purse or bag)
- ✔ **varyezhki** (*vah*-reesh-kee; mittens)
- ✔ **zontik** (*zohn*-teek; umbrella)

In the store called **muzhkaya odyezhda** (moosh-*skah-yuh ah d'ulrzh*-duh; men's apparel), you can find the following:

- ✔ **bryuki** (*bryu*-kee; pants)
- ✔ **dzhinsy** (*dzhihn*-sih; jeans)
- ✔ **futbolka** (foot-*bohl*-kuh; football jersey/sports shirt)
- ✔ **kostyum** (kahs-*tyum;* suit)
- ✔ **maika** (*mahy*-kuh; T-shirt)
- ✔ **pidzhak** (peed-*zhahk;* suit jacket)
- ✔ **plavki** (*plahf*-kee; swimming trunks)
- ✔ **rubashka** (roo-*bahsh*-kuh; shirt)
- ✔ **shorty** (*shohr*-tih; shorts)
- ✔ **svitehr** (*svee*-tehr; sweater)
- ✔ **trusy** (troo-*sih;* men's underwear)
- ✔ **zhilyet** (zhih-*l'eht;* vest)

In the store **zhyensaya odyezhda** (*zhehn*-skuh-yuh ah-*d'ehzh*-duh; women's apparel), you can find a

- ✔ **bluzka** (*bloos*-kuh; blouse)
- ✔ **kofta** (*kohf*-tuh; cardigan)
- ✔ **lifchik** (*leef*-cheek; bra)
- ✔ **plat'ye** (*plah*-t'yeh; dress)
- ✔ **sarafan** (suh-ruh-*fahn;* sleeveless dress)
- ✔ **yubka** (*yup*-kuh; skirt)
- ✔ **zhenskoye byel'yo** (*zhehn*-skuh-eh beel'-yo; women's underwear)

And if you need a hat, drop by the store or department called **golovnyye ubory** (guh-lahv-*nih*-ye oo-*boh*-rih; hats) and buy a

- ✔ **kyepka** (*k'ehp*-kuh; cap)
- ✔ **platok** (pluh-*tohk;* head scarf)
- ✔ **shapka** (*shahp*-kuh; warm winter hat)

✔ **sharf** (shahrf; scarf)

✔ **shlyapa** (shl'ah-puh; hat)

Describing items in color

What's your favorite color? When picking out clothes, you may want to tell the salesperson **Ya lyublyu krasnyj tsvyet** (ya l'oob-*l'oo* krahs-nihy tsveht; I like red [*literally:* I like the color red]) or **Ya lyublyu zyelyonyj tsvyet** (ya lyub-*lyu* zee-*lyo*-nihy tsveht; I like green [*literally:* I like the color green]). Some common colors are

✔ **byelyj** (*b'eh*-lihy; white)

✔ **chyornyj** (*chyor*-nihy; black)

✔ **goluboj** (guh-loo-*bohy;* light blue)

✔ **korichnyevyj** (kah-*reech*-nee-vihy; brown)

✔ **krasnyj** (*krahs*-nihy; red)

✔ **oranzhyevyj** (ah-*rahn*-zhih-vihy; orange)

✔ **purpurnyj** (poor-*poor*-nihy; purple)

✔ **rozovyj** (*roh*-zuh-vihy; pink)

✔ **siniy** (*see*-neey; blue)

✔ **syeryj** (*s'eh*-rihy; gray)

✔ **zhyoltyj** (*zhohl*-tihy; yellow)

✔ **zyelyonyj** (zee-*lyo*-nihy; green)

The names for colors in Russian are considered adjectives. So when you're describing the color of an item you want, make sure the color agrees in case, number, and gender with the noun it modifies. (For more on adjective-noun agreement, see Chapter 2.) For example, a black hat in the nominative case is **chyornaya shlyapa** (*chohr*-nuh-yuh *shl'ah*-puh), a black dress is **chyornoye plat'ye** (*chohr*-nuh-eh *plaht'*-yeh), and black shoes are **chyornyye botinki** (*chohr*-nih-eh bah-*tehn*-keh).

If you want to ask for a different shade of a color, use the phrase **A potyemnyeye/posvyetlyye yest'?** (uh puh-teem-*n'eh*-eh/puhs-veet-*l'eh-eh yest'?*; Do you have it in a darker/lighter shade?). Other words that may come in handy are **odnotsvyetnyj** (uhd-nah-*tsveht*-nihy; solid), and **raznotsvyetnyj** (ruhz-nah-*tsveht*-nihy; patterned).

Finding the right size

Here are some of the words and phrases you may hear or say while searching for your right size:

▸ **Razmehr** (ruhz-*m'ehr;* size)

▸ **Ya noshu razmyer . . .** (ya nah-*shoo* ruhz-*m'ehr;* I wear size . . .)

▸ **Eto moj razmyer.** (*eh*-tuh mohy ruhz-*m'ehr;* This is my size.)

▸ **Kakoj vash/u vas razmyer?** (kuh-*kohy* vahsh/oo vahs ruhz-*m'ehr?;* What's your size?)

Trying on clothing

Before you decide you want to **nosit'** (nah-seet; wear) something, you probably want to try it on first. To ask to try something on, you say **Mozhno pomyerit'?** (*mohzh*-nuh pah-*m'eh*-reet'?; May I try this on?). You'll most likely hear **Da, pozhalujsta** (dah, pah-*zhah*-luh-stuh; Yes, please).

When you try something on, and it fits you well, you say **Eto khorosho sidit** (*eh*-tuh khuh-rah-*shoh* see-*deet;* It fits). If it doesn't fit, you say **Eto plohkho sidit** (*eh*-tuh *ploh*-khuh see-*deet;* It doesn't fit). Here are some other adjectives you may use to describe the clothes you're considering buying:

▸ **khoroshyj** (khah-*roh-shihy;* good)

▸ **plokhoj** (plah-*khohy;* bad)

▸ **bol'shoj** (bahl'-*shohy;* big)

- ✔ **malyenkij** (*mah*-leen'-keey; small)
- ✔ **dlinnyi** (*dlee*-nihy; long)
- ✔ **korotkij** (kah-*roht*-keey; short)

Don't forget when using these adjectives to add the correct ending, which depends on the case, number, and gender of the noun the adjective refers to. (For more on adjective-noun agreement, see Chapter 2.)

The item you've just tried on may turn out to be too big or too small. To say something is too big, use this construction: The name of the item + **mnye** (mn'eh; to me) followed by

- ✔ **vyelik** (vee-*leek;* too big) for masculine nouns
- ✔ **vyelika** (vee-lee-*kah;* too big) for feminine nouns
- ✔ **vyeliko** (vee-lee-*koh;* too big) for neuter nouns
- ✔ **vyeliki** (vee-lee-*kee;* too big) for plural nouns

If the raincoat you just tried on is too big, for example, you say **Etot plash' mnye vyelik** (*eh*-tuht plahsh' mn'eh vee-*leek;* This raincoat is too big for me).

If, on the other hand, something is too small, you say the name of the item + **mnye** + one of the following:

- ✔ **mal** (mahl; too small) for masculine nouns
- ✔ **mala** (muh-*lah;* too small) for feminine nouns
- ✔ **malo** (muh-*loh;* too small) for neuter nouns
- ✔ **maly** (muh-*lih;* too small) for plural nouns

This or That? Deciding What You Want

The blue dress or the black pants. How do you decide? Can't help you there, but this section helps you discuss your dilemma.

Expressing likes and dislikes

When people go shopping, they often base their final
decisions on one simple thing: You either like something or you don't! To express that you like something
in Russian, you say **Mnye** (mn'eh; *literally:* to me) + a
form of the verb **nravitsya** (*nrah*-veet-s'eh; to like) +
the thing(s) you like. The verb must agree in number
(and gender, for past tense) with the thing(s) you like.
It's a peculiar construction: What you're saying literally is "To me, something is liked." If you like a particular coat, for example, you say **Mnye nravitsya eta
kurtka** (mn'eh *nrah*-veet-s'uh *eh*-tuh *koort*-kuh; I like
this coat).

Table 6-1 has some other forms of the verb **nravitsya**
you may need to use, depending on the thing(s)
you're talking about and the tense you're using.

Table 6-1	Tenses of Nravit'sya
Tense	*Verb*
Present	**nravit'sya** (singular)
	nravyatsya (plural)
Past	**nravilsya** (masculine)
	narvilas' (feminine)
	nravilos' (neuter)
	naravilis' (plural)
Future	**budyet nravit'sya** (singular)
	budut nravit'sya (plural)

If you want to express that you *don't* like something,
you simply add **nye** (nee; not) before **nravitsya,** as in
Mnye nye nravitsya eta kurtka (mnye nee *nrah*-veet-
sye *eh*-tuh *koort*-kuh; I don't like this coat).

Comparing two items

To compare things, Russian uses comparative adjectives like **bol'shye** (*bohl'*-sheh; bigger), **myen'shye** (*m'ehn'*-sheh; smaller), **luchshye** (*looch*-sheh; better), and **khuzhye** (*khoo*-zheh; worse). Just as in English, you say the name of the item + the comparative adjectives (for instance, bigger or smaller) + the word **chyem** (chyem; than) + the other item. And here's some good news: Comparative adjectives do *not* need to agree in case, number, and gender with the nouns they refer to. They use the same form for every noun.

Say you're trying on two pairs of shoes. You like the second pair better: It's more comfortable, lighter, and cheaper, too. This is what you may be thinking to yourself: **Eti tufli udobnyeye, lyegchye, i dyeshyev-lye chyem tye** (*eh*-tee toof-lee oo-*dohb*-n'eh-eh *l'ehkh*-cheh ee dee-*shehv*-l'eh chyem tye; These shoes are more comfortable, lighter, and cheaper than those).

In addition to the words we use here, here are some other commonly used comparative adjectives in Russian:

- **dlinnyeye** (dl'eh-*nye*-eh; longer)
- **dorozhye** (dah-*roh*-zheh; more expensive)
- **dyeshyevlye** (dee-*shehv*-l'eh; cheaper)
- **intyeryesnyeye** (een-tee-*r'ehs*-n'eh-eh; more interesting)
- **kholodnyeye** (khuh-lahd-*n'eh*-eh; colder)
- **korochye** (kah-*rohch*-cheh; shorter)
- **krasivyeye** (kruh-*seh*-v'eh-eh; more beautiful)
- **tolsh'ye** (*tohl*-sh'e; thicker)
- **ton'shye** (*tohn'*-sheh; thinner)
- **tyazhyelyeye** (tee-zhih-*l'eh*-eh; heavier)
- **tyeplyeye** (teep-*l'eh*-eh; warmer)

Talking about what you like most (or least)

When you look at several items (or people or things), you may like one of them most of all. To communicate this preference, you need to use the superlative form of the adjective. Just like in English, Russian simply adds the word **samyj** (*sah*-mihy; the most) before the adjective and noun you're talking about.

To express the superlative form of the adjective, put **samyj** before the neutral adjective form, not the comparative adjective form, as given in the previous section. For a list of superlative adjective forms, see Table 6-2.

Samyj is an adjective and must agree in case, number, and gender with the nouns and other adjectives it modifies. (For details on adjective-noun agreement, see Chapter 2.) Table 6-2 has the forms of **samyj** you need to use.

Table 6-2	Speaking in Superlatives		
	Masculine	*Feminine*	*Neuter*
Singular	**samyj** (*sah*-mihy)	**samaya** (*sah*-muh-yuh)	**samoye** (*sah*-muh-yuh)
Plural	**samyye** (*sah*-mih-eh)	**samyye** (*sah*-mih-eh)	**samyye** (*sah*-mih-eh)

If one coat is the lightest of all the coats you tried on, you may want to say **Eta kurtka samaya lyogkaya** (*eh*-tuh *koort*-kuh *sah*-muh-ye *lyohk*-kuh-ye; This coat is the lightest). If you're particularly fond of one pair of earrings, you can say **Eti syer'gi samyye krasivyye** (*eh*-tee *syer'*-gee *sah*-mih-eh krah-*see*-vih-eh; These earrings are the most beautiful ones).

To communicate that something is the worst in its category, Russians today use the word **samyj plokhoj** (*sah-mihy plah-khohy* worst [*literally:* most bad]) for masculine nouns, **samaya plokhaya** (*sah-muh-yuh plah-khah-yuh*) for feminine nouns, **samoye plokhoye** (*sah-muh-eh plah-khoh-eh*) for neuter nouns, and **samyye plokhiye** (*sah-mih-eh plah-khee-eh*) for plural nouns.

So if you particularly dislike one dress, you say **Eto plat'ye samoye plokhoye** (eh-tuh *plah-*t'yeh *sah-*muh-eh plah-*khoh*-eh; That dress is the worst [*literally:* That dress is the most bad]).

You Gotta Pay to Play

To inquire about the price of any item, ask **Skol'ko stoit . . . ?** (*skohl'*-kuh *stoh*-eet . . . ?; How much does . . . cost?). After you hear the price, you may want to specify your question to avoid the confusion:

- **Za kilogram?** (zuh kee-lahg-*rahm;* Per kilo?)
- **Za shtuku?** (zuh *shtoo*-koo; Per item?)
- **Za yash'ik?** (zuh *ya*-sh'eek; Per box?)

When you're buying several items or paying for your meal at a restaurant, a good phrase to use is **Skol'ko s myenya?** (*skohl'*-kuh s mee-*n'ah;* How much do I owe?) Here are some other good phrases:

- **Eto ochyen' dorogo.** (*eh-*tuh *oh*-cheen' *doh*-ruh-guh; It's very expensive.)
- **Eto dyoshyevo!** (*eh-*tuh *dyo*-shih-vuh; It's cheap!)
- **Ya voz'mu eto.** (ya vahz'-*moo eh-*tuh; I'll take it.)
- **Ya eto kuplyu.** (ya *eh-*tuh koo-*pl'oo;* I'll buy it.)

Chapter 7

Making Leisure a Top Priority

. . . .

In This Chapter

▶ Planning to go out

▶ Sharing your impressions about an event

▶ Discussing your hobbies

▶ Reading everything

▶ Enjoying nature

▶ Collecting things, working with your hands, and playing sports

. . . .

*T*his chapter is all about leisure, whether going out on the town the Russian way or playing sports. And with the phrases you find here, you won't be short on words.

Together Wherever We Go: Making Plans to Go Out

Going out on the town with friends is always more fun. Here we give you all the words and expressions you need to invite your friends out with you, and we tell you how to accept or decline invitations you receive. We also tell you how to find out what time an event starts.

Here are common phrases people use to invite you to do things with them:

- **Pojdyom v . . .** (pahy-*dyom* v . . . , Let's go to the . . . [informal])

- **Pojdyomtye v . . .** (pahy-*dyom*-tye v . . . ; Let's go to the . . . [formal or plural])

- **Davaj pojdyom v . . .** (duh-*vahy* pahy-*dyom* v . . . ; Let's go to the . . . [informal])

- **Davajtye pojdyom v . . .** (duh-*vahy*-tye pahy-*dyom* v . . . ; Let's go to the . . . [formal or plural])

- **Ty khochyesh' pojti v . . .** (tih *khoh*-chehsh' pahy-*tee* v . . . ; Do you want to go to the . . . [informal])

- **Vy khotitye pojti v . . .** (vih khah-*tee*-tye pahy-*tee* v . . . ; Do you want to go to the . . . [formal or plural])

To let everybody around know that you want to go somewhere tonight, you may say **Ya khochu pojti v . . . syegodnya vyechyerom** (ya khah-*choo* pahy-*tee* f . . . see-*vohd*-nye *vye*-cheh-ruhm; I want to go to the . . . tonight).

After you ask someone to make plans with you (or after someone asks you), the big question is whether to decline or accept.

Russians don't easily take **nyet** for an answer! So if you need to decline an invitation, we recommend softening your response with one of the following:

- **K sozhalyeniyu, ya nye mogu.** (k suh-zhuh-*lye*-nee-yu ya nee mah-*goo;* Unfortunately, I can't.)

- **Ochyen' zhal', no ya v etot dyen' zanyat.** (*oh*-chyen' zhahl' noh ya v *eh*-tuht dyen' *zah*-neet; I am very sorry, but I am busy that day.)

- **Mozhyet byt', v drugoj dyen'?** (*moh*-zhiht biht' v droo-*gohy* dyen'?; Maybe on a different day?)

✔ **Mozhyet, luchshye pojdyom v kafye?** (*moh*-zhiht *looch*-shih pahy-*dyohm* f kah-*feh?;* Maybe we could go to a coffee shop instead?)

Here are some ways to spice up your **da:**

✔ **Spasibo, s udovol'stviyem!** (spah-*see*-buh s oo-dah-*vohl'*-stvee-eem!; Thank you, I would be happy to!)

✔ **Bol'shoye spasibo, ya obyazatyel'no pridu.** (bahl'-*shoh*-eh spuh-*see*-buh, ya ah-bee-*zah*-teel'-nuh pree-*doo;* Thank you very much, I'll come by all means.)

✔ **Spasibo, a kogda? Vo skol'ko?** (spah-*see*-buh ah kahg-*dah?* vah *skohl'*-kuh?; Thank you, and when? What time?)

Going Out on the Town

Whether going out with friends or family, you have lots of options for your weekend entertainment.

On the big screen: Going to the movies

Feel like seeing a **fil'm** (feel'm; movie) this weekend? Whereas English just uses the word *theater* for a movie theater, Russian is more exact in expressing the difference between a movie theater and a play, opera, or ballet theater. The word **kino** (kee-*noh*) or the more formal **kinotyeatr** (kee-nuh-tee-*ahtr*) are the only words you can use to denote *movie theater* in Russian.

Check out the following list for the names of different film genres in Russian:

✔ **dyetyektiv** (deh-tehk-*teef;* detective film)

✔ **ekranizatsiya khudozhyestvyennoj lityeratury** (eh-kruh-nee-*zah*-tsih-ye khoo-*doh*-zhihs-tvee-nuhy lee-tee-ruh-*too*-rih; screen version of a book)

✔ **fil'm uzhasov** (feel'm *oo*-zhuh-suhf; horror film)

- ✔ **komyediya** (kah-*mye*-dee-ye; comedy)
- ✔ **mul'tfil'm** (mool't-*feel'm;* cartoon)
- ✔ **myuzikl** (*m yu*-zeekl, musical)
- ✔ **nauhcnaya fantastika** (nuh-*ooch*-nuh-ye fuhn-*tahs*-tee-kuh; science fiction)
- ✔ **priklyuchyenchyeskij** fil'm (pree-klyu-*chyen*-chees-keey feel'm; adventure film)
- ✔ **trillyer** (*tree*-lyer; thriller)
- ✔ **vyestyern** (*vehs*-tehrn; western)

If you decide to go to the movies, you need a **bilyet** (bee-*lyet;* ticket). To ask for a ticket, customers often use a kind of a stenographic language. **Kassiry** (kuh-*see*-rih; cashiers) are generally impatient people, and you may have a line behind you. So try to make your request for a ticket as brief as you can. If you want to go to the 2:30 p.m. show, you say one of these phrases:

- ✔ **Odin na chyetyrnadtsat' tridtsat'.** (ah-*deen* nah chee-*tihr*-nuh-tsuht' *treet*-tsuht'; One for 2:30.)
- ✔ **Dva na chyetyrnadtsat' tridtsat'.** (dvah nah chee-*tihr*-nuh-tsuht' *treet*-tsuht'; Two for 2:30.)

It's classic: Taking in the Russian ballet and theater

If a Russian ballet company happens to be in your area, don't miss it! And if you're in Russia, don't even think of leaving without seeing at least one performance either in Moscow's Bol'shoy Theater or St. Petersburg's Mariinski Theater. No ballet in the world can compare with the Russian **balyet** (buh-*lyet;* ballet) in its grand, powerful style; lavish décor; impeccable technique; and proud preservation of the classical tradition.

The Russian **teatr** (tee-*ahtr;* theater) is just as famous and impressive as the ballet, but most theater performances are in Russian, so you may not understand a lot until you work on your Russian for a while. Still, if you want to see great acting and test your Russian knowledge, by all means check out the theater, too!

When you buy tickets, you may hear **Gdye vy khoti-tye sidyet'?** (gdye vih khah-*tee*-tee see-*dyet'?;* Where do you want to sit?) or **Kakoj ryad?** (kah-*kohy* ryat?; Which row?). If you prefer a centrally located seat, you say **V partyerye** (f puhr-*teh*-ree; In the orchestra seats). Here are some other seating options you may want to consider, depending on your budget and taste:

- ✔ **lozha** (*loh*-zhuh; box seat)
- ✔ **byenuar** (bee-noo-*ahr;* lower boxes)
- ✔ **byel'etazh** (behl'-eh-*tahsh;* tier above **byenuar**)
- ✔ **yarus** (*ya*-roos; tier above **bel'ehtazh**)
- ✔ **galyeryeya** (guh-lee-*rye*-ye; the last balcony)
- ✔ **balkon** (buhl-*kohn;* balcony)

During the **antrakt** (uhn-*trahkt;* intermission), take a walk around the **koridor** (kuh-ree-*dohr;* hall) and look at the pictures of the past and current **aktyory** (uhk-*tyo*-rih; actors), **aktrisy** (uhk-*tree*-sih; actresses), **balyeriny** (buh-lee-*ree*-nih; ballerinas), and **rezhissy-ory** (ree-zhih-*syo*-rih; theater directors) that are usually displayed. Another thing you may want to do is grab a bite to eat at the **bufyet** (boo-*fyet;* buffet), which is designed to make you feel that coming to the theater is a very special occasion. Typical buffet delicacies are: **butyerbrod s ikroj** (boo-tehr-*broht* s eek-*rohy;* a caviar sandwich), **butyerbrod s kopchyonoj ryboj** (boo-tehr-*broht* s kuhp-*chyo*-nuhy *rih*-buhy; a smoked fish sandwich), **pirozhnyye** (pee-*rozh*-nih-ee; pastries), **shokolad** (shuh-kah-*laht;* chocolate), and **shampanskoye** (shuhm-*pahn*-skuh-ye; champagne).

Culture club: Visiting a museum

Russians are a nation of museum-goers. Visiting a **muzyej** (moo-*zyey;* museum) is seen as a "culture" trip. In almost every city, you're likely to find the following museums to satisfy your hunger for culture:

- **Etnografichyeskij muzyej** (eht-nuh-gruh-*fee*-chees-keey moo-*zyey;* ethnographic museum)

- **Istorichyeskij muzyej** (ee-stah-*ree*-chees-keey moo-*zyey;* historical museum)

- **Kartinnaya galyeryeya** (kuhr-*tee*-nuh-ya guh-lee-*rye*-ya; art gallery)

- **Muzyej istorii goroda** (moo-*zyey* ees-*toh*-ree-ee *goh*-ruh-duh; museum of the town history)

- **Muzyej istorii kraya** (moo-*zyey* ees-*toh*-ree-ee *krah*-ya; regional history museum)

Also, you may want to visit any of the large number of Russian museums dedicated to famous and not-so-famous Russian **pisatyeli** (pee-*sah*-tye-lee; writers), **poety** (pah-*eh*-tih; poets), **aktyory** (uhk-*tyo*-rih; actors) and **aktrisy** (uhk-*tree*-sih; actresses), **khudozhniki** (khoo-*dohzh*-nee-kee; artists), **uchyonyye** (oo-*choh*-nih-ye; scientists), and **politiki** (pah-*lee*-tee-kee; politicians). For example, in St. Petersburg alone, you find the A. S. Pushkin museum, the F. M. Dostoyevsky museum, A. A. Akhmatova museum, and many, many more — almost enough for every weekend of the year!

Some other words and expressions you may need in a museum are

- **ekskursant** (ehks-koor-*sahnt;* member of a tour group)

- **ekskursiya** (ihks-*koor*-see-ya; tour)

- **ekskursovod** (ihks-koor-sah-*voht;* guide)

- **eksponat** (ihks-pah-*naht;* exhibit)

- **ekspozitsiya** (ihks-pah-*zee*-tsih-ye; display)

- **iskusstvo** (ees-*koos*-tvuh; arts)

- **kartina** (kuhr-*tee*-nuh; painting)

✔ **putyevodityel'** (poo-tee-vah-*dee*-teel'; guidebook)

✔ **skul'ptura** (skool'-*ptoo*-ruh; sculpture or piece of sculpture)

✔ **vystavka** (*vihs*-tuhf-kuh; exhibition)

✔ **zal** (zahl; exhibition hall)

✔ **Muzyyej otkryvayetsya v . . .** (moo-*zyey* uht-krih-*vah*-eet-suh v . . . ; The museum opens at . . .)

✔ **Muzyyej zakryvayetsya v . . .** (moo-*zyey* zuh-krih-*vah*-eet-suh v . . . ; The museum closes at . . .)

✔ **Skol'ko stoyat vkhodnyye bilyety?** (*skohl'*-kuh *stoh*-eet fkhahd-*nih*-ee bee-*lye*-tih?; How much do admission tickets cost?)

Shootin' the Breeze about Hobbies

Before getting to the nitty-gritty of your **khobbi** (*khoh*-bee; hobby or hobbies — the word is used for both singular and plural forms), you probably want to test the water so that you don't exhaust your vocabulary of Russian exclamations discussing Tchaikovsky with someone who prefers boxing. To discover someone's likes or dislikes, you can ask one of the following:

✔ **Chyem ty lyubish' zanimat'sya?** (chyem tih *lyu*-beesh' zuh-nee-*maht*-suh?; What do you like to do? [informal singular])

✔ **Chyem vy lyubitye zanimat'sya?** (chyem vih *lyu*-bee-tee zuh-nee-*maht*-suh?; What do you like to do? [formal singular; plural])

✔ **Ty lyubish' . . . ?** (tih *lyu*-beesh' . . . ?; Do you like . . . ? [informal singular]) + the imperfective infinitive of a verb or a noun in the accusative case (see Chapter 2)

✔ **Vy lyubitye . . . ?** (vih *lyu*-bee-tee . . . ?; Do you like . . . ? [formal singular; plural]) + the imperfective infinitive of a verb or a noun in the accusative case (see Chapter 2)

You use the verb **lyubit'** (lyu-*beet';* to love or to like) to describe your feelings toward almost anything, from **borsh'** (borsh'; bor-shcht) to your significant other. Saying **Ya lyublyu gruppu U2** (ya lyu-*blyu* groo-poo yu-*too;* I like the band U2) isn't too strong, and this word is just right to express your feelings for your family members, too: **Ya lyublyu moyu malyen'kuyu syestru** (ya lyu-*blyu* mah-*yu mah*-leen'-koo-yu sees-*troo;* I love my little sister).

Table 7-1 shows you how to conjugate the verb **lyubit'** in the present tense.

Table 7-1	Conjugation of Lyubit'	
Conjugation	*Pronunciation*	*Translation*
ya lyublyu	yah lyu-*blyu*	I love/like
ty lyubish'	tih *lyu*-beesh'	You love/like (informal singular)
on/ona/ ono lyubit'	on/ah-*nah*/ ah-*noh* lyu-byet'	He/she/it loves/likes
my lyubim	mih *lyu*-beem	We love/like
vy lyubitye	vih *lyu*-bee-tye	You love/like (formal singular; plural)
oni lyubyat	ah-*nee lyu*-byet	They love/like

Reading All About It

An American who has traveled in Russia observed that, on the Moscow metro, half the people are reading books and the other half are holding beer bottles. But we don't agree with such a sharp division. Some Russians can be holding a book in one hand and a beer bottle in the other! But, all joking aside, Russians are still reported to read more than any other nation in the world. So, get prepared to discuss your reading habits.

Have you read it?

When you talk about reading, a handy verb to know is **chitat'** (chee-*taht'*; to read). This verb is a regular verb. Here are some essential phrases you need in a conversation about reading:

- ✔ **Ya chitayu . . .** (ya chee-*tah*-yu . . . ; I read/am reading . . .) + a noun in the accusative case

- ✔ **Chto ty chitayesh'?** (shtoh tih chee-*tah*-yesh'?; What are you reading? [informal singular])

- ✔ **Chto vy chitayetye?** (shtoh vih chee-*tah*-ee-tye?; What are you reading? [formal singular; plural])

- ✔ **Ty chital . . . ?** (tih chee-*tahl* . . . ?; Have you read . . . ? [informal singular]) + a noun in the accusative case when speaking to a male

- ✔ **Ty chitala . . . ?** (tih chee-*tah*-luh . . . ?; Have you read . . . ? [informal singular]) + a noun in the accusative case when speaking to a female

- ✔ **Vy chitali . . . ?** (vih chee-*tah*-lee . . . ?; Have you read . . . ? [formal singular; plural]) + a noun in the accusative case

What do you like to read?

So you're ready to talk about your favorite **kniga** (*knee*-guh; book) or **knigi** (*knee*-gee; books). Here are some words to outline your general preferences in literature, some of which may sound very familiar:

- ✔ **lityeratura** (lee-tee-ruh-*too*-ruh; literature)

- ✔ **povyesti** (*poh*-vees-tee; tales)

- ✔ **poyeziya** (pah-*eh*-zee-ye; poetry)

- ✔ **proza** (*proh*-zuh; prose)

- ✔ **p'yesy** (*p'ye*-sih; plays)

- ✔ **rasskazy** (ruhs-*kah*-zih; short stories)

✔ **romany** (rah-*mah*-nih; novels)

✔ **stikhi** (stee-*khee*; poems)

The conversation probably doesn't end with your saying **Ya lyublyu chitat' romany** (ya lyu-*blyu* chee-*taht'* rah-*mah*-nih; I like to read novels). Somebody will ask you: **A kakiye romany vy lyubitye?** (ah kuh-*kee*-ee rah-*mah*-nih vih *lyu*-bee-tee?; And what kind of novels do you like?). To answer this question, you can simply say **Ya lyublyu . . .** (ya lyu-*blyu*; I like . . .) + one of the following genres:

✔ **biografii** (bee-ahg-*rah*-fee-ee; biographies)

✔ **boyeviki** (buh-ee-vee-*kee*; action novels)

✔ **dyetyektivy** (deh-tehk-*tee*-vih; mysteries)

✔ **fantastika** (fuhn-*tahs*-tee-kuh; science fiction)

✔ **istorichyeskiye isslyedovaniya** (ees-tah-*ree*-chees-kee-ye ees-*lye*-duh-vuh-nee-ye; history [*literally:* historical research])

✔ **istorichyeskaya proza** (ees-tah-*ree*-chees-kuh-ye *proh*-zuh; historical fiction)

✔ **lyubovnyye romany** (lyu-*bohv*-nih-ee rah-*mah*-nih; romance)

✔ **myemuary** (meh-moo-*ah*-rih; memoirs)

✔ **sovryemyennaya proza** (suhv-ree-*mye*-nuh-ye *proh*-zuh; contemporary fiction)

✔ **trillyery** (*tree*-lee-rih; thrillers)

✔ **vyestyerny** (*vehs*-tehr-nih; Westerns)

Now you're well-prepared to talk about literature, but what about the news, political commentary, and celebrity gossip? These phrases can help:

✔ **gazyeta** (guh-*zye*-tuh; newspaper)

✔ **komiksy** (*koh*-meek-sih; comic books)

✔ **novosti** (*noh*-vuhs-tee; the news)

✔ **novosti v intyernyetye** (*noh*-vuhs-tee v een-tehr-*neh*-tye; news on the Internet)

✔ **stat'ya** (stuh-*t'ya;* article)

✔ **zhurnal** (zhoor-*nahl;* magazine)

Rejoicing in the Lap of Nature

Russians love nature. Every city in Russia has big parks where numerous urban dwellers take walks, enjoy picnics, and swim in suspiciously smelling ponds. Even more so, Russians like to get out of town and enjoy the nature in the wild. Luckily, the country's diverse geography offers a wide variety of opportunities to do so. In the following sections, you discover how to make the most out of enjoying nature in Russian.

Enjoying the country house

The easiest route to nature is through the **dacha** (*dah*-chuh), which is a little country house not far from the city that most Russians have. **Poyekhat' na dachu** (pah-*ye*-khuht' nuh *dah*-choo; to go to the dacha) usually implies an overnight visit that includes barbecuing, dining in the fresh air, and, if you're lucky, **banya** (*bah*-nye) — the Russian-style sauna. Some phrases to use during your **dacha** experience include the following:

✔ **natopit' banyu** (nuh-tah-*peet' bah*-nyu; to prepare the sauna)

✔ **ogorod** (uh-gah-*roht;* vegetable garden)

✔ **rabotat' v sadu** (ruh-*boh*-tuht' f suh-*doo;* to garden)

✔ **razvodit' kostyor** (ruhz-vah-*deet'* kahs-*tyor;* to make a campfire)

✔ **sad** (saht; orchard or garden)

✔ **sobirat' ovosh'i** (suh-bee-*raht' oh*-vuh-sh'ee; to pick vegetables)

✔ **zharit' shashlyk** (*zhah*-reet' shuh-*shlihk;* to barbecue)

Skiing in the Caucasus

The Caucasus, a picturesque mountainous region in the South of Russia, is easily accessible by train or by a flight into the city of Minvody. The best places to ski in the Caucasus (called **Kavkaz** in Russian) include **Dombaj** (dahm-*bahy*) and **Priyel'brus'ye** (pree-ehl'-*broo*-s'ee). The word **Priel'brus'ye** actually means "next to El'brus," with **El'brus** (ehl'-*broos*) being the highest mountain peak in Europe (according to those who consider the Caucasus a part of Europe).

Here are some phrases to help you organize your skiing adventure:

- **gora** (gah-*rah;* mountain)
- **gory** (*goh*-rih; mountains)
- **kanatka** (kuh-*naht*-kuh; informal for cable cars)
- **kanatnaya doroga** (kuh-*naht*-nuh-ye dah-*roh*-guh; cable cars)
- **katat'sya na lyzhakh** (kuh-*taht'*-suh nuh *lih*-zhuhkh; to ski)
- **kryem ot zagara** (krehm uht zuh-*gah*-ruh; sunblock)
- **lyzhi** (*lih*-zhih; skis)
- **prokat** (prah-*kaht;* rental)
- **snoubord** (snoh-oo-*bohrd;* snowboard)
- **turbaza** (toor-*bah*-zuh; tourist center)
- **vzyat' na prokat** (vzyat' nuh prah-*kaht;* to rent)

Lying around at Lake Baikal

With its picturesque cliffs, numerous islands, and crystal clear water, **Ozyero Baikal** (*oh*-zee-ruh buhy-*kahl;* Lake Baikal) is an unforgettable vacation spot. Having these words at your disposal makes your experience more enjoyable:

- ✔ **bajdarka** (buhy-*dahr*-kuh; kayak)
- ✔ **byeryeg** (*bye*-ryek; shore)
- ✔ **katyer** (*kah*-tyer; boat)
- ✔ **komary** (kuh-muh-*rih;* mosquitoes)
- ✔ **lovit' rybu** (lah-*veet' rih*-boo; to fish)
- ✔ **ostrov** (*ohs*-truhf; island)
- ✔ **parom** (puh-*rohm;* ferry)
- ✔ **plavat'** (*plah*-vuht'; to swim)
- ✔ **plyazh** (plyash; beach)
- ✔ **prichal** (pree-*chahl;* pier)
- ✔ **pristan'** (*prees*-tuhn'; loading dock)
- ✔ **ryechnoj vokzal** (reech-*nohy* vahk-*zahl;* marina)
- ✔ **port** (pohrt; port)
- ✔ **rybalka** (rih-*bahl*-kuh; fishing)

Doing Things with Your Hands

Exploring natural wonders and architectural gems is fun, but so is discovering your internal treasures. In the following sections, you find out how to talk about nifty things you can do with your hands. Don't be shy — your **talant** (tuh-*lahnt;* talent) deserves to be talked about!

Being crafty

If you're one of those lucky people who can create things with your hands, use the following words to describe your craft:

- ✔ **dyelat' loskutnyye odyeyala** (*dye*-luht' luhs-*koot*-nih-ee uh-dee-*ya*-luh; to quilt)
- ✔ **lyepit'** (lee-*peet';* to sculpt)
- ✔ **lyepit' iz gliny** (lee-*peet'* eez *glee*-nih; to make pottery)

✔ **pisat' maslom** (pee-*saht' mahs*-luhm; to paint)

✔ **risovat'** (ree-sah-*vaht';* to draw)

✔ **shit** (shiiit ; to sew)

✔ **vyazat'** (veeh-*zaht';* to knit)

To ask someone whether he or she can do one of these crafts, use the verb **umyet'** (oo-myet'; can) plus the infinitive:

✔ **Ty umyeyesh pisat' maslom?** (tih oo-*mye*-yesh' pee-*saht' mahs*-luhm?; Can you paint? [informal singular])

✔ **Vy umyeyetye vyazat'?** (vih oo-*mye*-ye-tye vee-*zaht'?;* Can you knit? [formal singular, plural])

To answer these kinds of questions, you can say:

✔ **Da, ya umyeyu.** (dah ya oo-*mye*-yu; Yes, I can.)

✔ **Nyet, ya nye umyeyu.** (nyet ya nee oo-*mye*-yu; No, I can't.)

Playing music

Do you like **muzyka** (*moo*-zih-kuh; music)? To talk about playing a **muzykal'nyj instrumyent** (moo-zih-*kahl'*-nihy een-stroo-*myent;* musical instrument), use the verb **igrat'** (eeg-*raht';* to play) + the preposition **na** (nah) and the name of the instrument in the prepositional case.

You can ask the following questions:

✔ **Ty umyeyesh' igrat' na . . . ?** (tih oo-*mye*-yesh' eeg-*raht'* nah . . . ?; Can you play . . . ? [informal singular]) + the name of the instrument in the prepositional case

✔ **Vy umyeyetye igrat' na . . . ?** (vih oo-*mye*-ee-tee eeg-*raht'* nah . . .?; Can you play . . . ? [formal singular; plural]) + the name of the instrument in the prepositional case

Some musical instruments you may want to mention include the following:

- ✔ **baraban** (buh-ruh-*bahn;* drum)
- ✔ **flyejta** (*flyey*-tuh; flute)
- ✔ **gitara** (gee-*tah*-ruh; guitar)
- ✔ **klarnyet** (kluhr-*nyet;* clarinet)
- ✔ **pianino** (pee-uh-*nee*-nuh; piano)
- ✔ **saksofon** (suhk-suh-*fohn;* saxophone)
- ✔ **skripka** (*skreep*-kuh; violin)
- ✔ **trombon** (trahm-*bohn;* trombone)
- ✔ **truba** (troo-*bah;* tuba)

Scoring with Sports

To talk about playing sports, use the verb **zanimat'sya** (zuh-nee-*maht'*-suh; to engage in or to play a sport). The name of the sport after this verb should be in the instrumental case. The word for *sports* is **sport** (spohrt); it's always singular.

Zanimat'sya is a reflexive verb. That means that at the end of it, you have a little **–sya** particle that remains there no matter how you conjugate the verb. This **–sya** particle is what remained of **syebya** (see-*bya;* oneself). The use of this particle directs the action onto the speaker. Thus, **zanimat'sya** means "to engage oneself." The same verb without the **–sya** particle, **zanimat'**, means "to engage somebody else." Reflexive verbs aren't very numerous in Russian — we warn you whenever we come across them.

You can ask somebody **Ty zanimayesh'sya sportom?** (tih zuh-nee-*mah*-yesh-suh *spohr*-tuhm?; Do you play sports? [*literally:* Do you engage in sports?]) You can answer this question by saying one of two phrases:

✔ **Da, ya zanimayus'** . . . (dah ya zuh-nee-*mah*-yus' . . . ; Yes, I play . . .) + the name of the sport in the instrumental case

✔ **Nyet, ya ne zanimayus' sportom.** (nyet ya nee zuh-nee-*mah*-yus' spohr-tuhm; No, I don't play sports.)

If you're talking about a team sport that can also be called an **igra** (eeg-*rah;* game), you can use the expression **igrat' v** (eeg-*raht'* v; to play) + the name of the sport in the accusative case. For instance: **Ty igrayesh' v futbol?** (tih eeg-*rah*-yesh' f foot-*bohl?;* Do you play soccer?)

Here's a list of sports you may want to talk about:

✔ **baskyetbol** (buhs-keet-*bohl;* basketball)

✔ **byejsbol** (beeys-*bohl;* baseball)

✔ **futbol** (foot-*bohl;* soccer)

✔ **gol'f** (gohl'f; golf)

✔ **tyennis** (*teh*-nees; tennis)

✔ **vollyejbol** (vuh-leey-*bohl;* volleyball)

To talk about watching a game, you can use the verb **smotryet** (smaht-*ryet';* to watch).

Chapter 8

When You Gotta Work

. . . .

In This Chapter

▶ Finding employment

▶ Making a phone call

▶ Sending a variety of written correspondence

. . . .

*W*hether you're looking for a job or just need to talk with your coworkers, this chapter has the phrases for you. We also give you basic phone vocabulary and tell you how to send letters, e-mails, and faxes.

Searching for a Job

A great Russian proverb summarizes Russians' attitude to work: **Rabota — nye volk, v lyes nye ubyezhit.** (ruh-*boh*-tuh — nee vohlk, v lyes nee oo-bee-*zhiht;* Work isn't a wolf, it won't run away from you into the forest.) In the following sections, you discover all you need to know about finding a job in Russia.

Discovering where to look

Looking for a job in Russia isn't much different from job-searching elsewhere in the world. Your options are

- ✔ Going to a **kadrovoye agyentstvo** (*kahd*-ruh-vuh-eh uh-*gyens*-tvuh; recruiting agency)

- ✔ Posting your **ryezyumye** (ree-zyu-*meh*; résumé) on a **sajt po poisku raboty** (sahjt pah *poh*-ees-koo ruh-*boh*-tih; job finder Web site)

- ✔ Looking for an **ob'yavlyeniye** (uhb-yeev-*lye*-nee-eh; announcement/ad) in a newspaper or a magazine

- ✔ Harassing your friends

If you decide to go with option two, there are three main online job sites: www.job.ru, www.rabota.ru, and www.headhunter.ru.

The most popular newspapers that offer employment information are ***Rabota dlya vas*** (ruh-*boh*-tuh dlya vahs; *Jobs for You*), ***Rabota i zarplata*** (ruh-*boh*-tuh ee zuhr-*plah*-tuh; *Jobs and Wages*), and ***Elitnyj pyersonal*** (eh-*leet*-nihy peer-sah-*nahl*; *Elite Personnel*).

Some phrases to look for when you're scanning the ads:

- ✔ **opyt raboty** (*oh*-piht ruh-*boh*-tih; experience in the field)

- ✔ **otpusk** (*oht*-poosk; vacation time)

- ✔ **ryekommyendatsii** (ree-kuh-meen-*dah*-tsih-ee; recommendations)

- ✔ **strakhovka** (struh-*khohf*-kuh; insurance)

- ✔ **vakansiya** (vuh-*kahn*-see-ye; vacancy)

- ✔ **zarplata** (zuhr-*plah*-tuh; wage)

Contacting employers

When you identify a **rabotodatyel'** (ruh-*boh*-tuh-*dah*-teel'; employer) that you're interested in, you want **poslat' ryezyumye** (pahs-*laht'* ree-zyu-*meh;* to send a résumé). You have several ways to do it; to find out which way is preferred by the employer, you can ask **Mnye prislat' ryezyumye . . .** (mnye prees-*laht'* ree-zyu-*meh;* Should I send my résumé . . .) + one of the following:

- ✔ **po faksu?** (puh fahksoo?; by fax)
- ✔ **po elektronnoj pochtye?** (puh ee-leek-*troh*-nuhy *pohch*-tee?; by e-mail)
- ✔ **po pochtye?** (puh *pohch*-tee?; by mail)

A Russian résumé, unlike an American one, includes your gender, birth date, and **syemye-jnoye polozhyeniye** (see-*myey*-nuh-ee puh-lah-*zheh*-nee-eh; marital status). Some employers may even ask you to include your picture!

The next step is an **intyerv'yu** (een-tehr-*v'yu;* interview). If you want to bring some supporting documents to the interview, but you aren't sure which ones to bring, you may want to ask **Kakiye dokumyenty mnye prinyesti na intyerv'yu?** (kuh-*kee*-eh duh-koo-*myen*-tih mnye pree-nees-*tee* nuh een-tehr-*v'yu?;* Which documents should I bring to the interview?) The answers can include

- ✔ **diplom** (deep-*lohm;* diploma)
- ✔ **razryeshyeniye na rabotu** (ruhz-ree-*sheh*-nee-eh nuh ruh-*boh*-too; work authorization)
- ✔ **ryekommyendatsiya** (ree-kuh-meen-*dah*-tsih-ye; reference)

Clarifying job responsibilities

To find out about your **obyazannosti** (ah-*bya*-zuh-nuhs-tee; job responsibilities), you need to ask questions. A good place to start is with the following question: **Chto vkhodit v moi obyazannosti?** (shtoh f *khoh*-deet v mah-*ee* ah-*bya*-zuh-nuhs-tee?; What do my job responsibilities include?)

The variety of professional skills is endless, but these words are likely to be useful:

- ✔ **pyechatat'** (pee-*chah*-tuht'; to type)

- ✔ **pyeryevodit'** (pee-ree-vah-*deet';* to translate)

- ✔ **rabotat' s komp'yutyerom** (ruh-*boh*-tuht' s kahm-p'*yoo*-teh-ruhm; to work with a computer)

Communicating in the Workplace

The thing about the workplace is that you're never alone. You often need to talk to a **kollyega** (kah-*lye*-guh; coworker), your **nachal'nik** (nuh-*chahl'*-neek; boss), or a **kliyent** (klee-*yent;* client). In the following sections, find out what to say in the workplace and how to say it in Russian.

Making an appointment

Here are the standard phrases used to **naznachit' vstryechu** (nuh-*znah*-cheet' *fstrye*-choo; make an appointment):

- ✔ **Davajtye vstryetimsya v dyevyat' chasov utra.** (duh-*vahy*-tee *fstrye*-teem-sye v *dye*-veet' chuh-*sohf* oo-*trah;* Let's meet at 9 a.m.)

- ✔ **Ya budu vas zhdat' v tri chasa dnya.** (ya *boo*-doo vahs zhdaht' f tree chuh-*sah* dnya; I'll be waiting for you at 3 p.m.)

If you're arranging for a phone call, you can say:

- ✔ **Ya budu zhdat' vashyego zvonka v dyesyat' chasov utra.** (ya *boo*-doo zhdaht' *vah*-shih-vuh zvahn-*kah* v *dye*-seet' chuh-*sohf* oo-*trah;* I'll be waiting for your phone call at 10 a.m.)

- ✔ **Ya vam pozvonyu v dva chasa dnya.** (ya vahm puh-zvah-*nyu* v dvah chuh-*sah* dnya; I'll call you at 2 p.m.)

Sticking to workplace etiquette

Russian business etiquette is not as strict as that of some other cultures. Just garnish your speech generously with **pozhalujsta** (pah-*zhah-luh*-stuh; please) and **spasibo** (spuh-*see*-buh; thank you), and you'll already sound more formal than an average Russian in the workplace.

The main thing you notice about Russian **dyelovoj etikyet** (dee-lah-*vohy* eh-tee-*kyet;* workplace etiquette) is that it's less formal than what you may be used to. Engaging in humorous exchanges that fall far from political correctness is considered normal, and your coworkers are likely to throw plenty of improvised parties at the office. Bosses and clients, however, are excluded from these friendly interactions, unless they decide to set the playful tone themselves.

Always use the formal **vy** (vih; you [formal singular and plural]) whenever you communicate with anyone in the workplace. If your coworkers and, especially, your boss, want to switch to less-formal terms, they'll tell you so. Wait for the initiative to come from them.

To avoid uncomfortable situations, always use the first name + patronymic form to address your colleagues. If they want you to switch to the Western first-name manner, they'll tell you: **Myenya mozhno zvat' prosto Sasha.** (mee-*nya mohzh*-nuh zvaht' *proh*-stuh *sah*-shuh; You can call me simply Sasha.) For more information on Russian names, see Chapter 3.

Here are some general polite phrases to use in the workplace:

> ✔ **Ya mogu vam chyem-nibud' pomoch'?** (ya mah-*goo* vahm *chehm*-nee-boot' pah-*mohch?;* Can I help you with anything?)

✔ **Bol'shoye spasibo, vy mnye ochyen' pomogli.**
(bahl'-*shoh*-eh spuh-*see*-buh, vih mnye *oh*-cheen'
puh-mahg-*lee;* Thank you very much, you
helped me a lot.)

Ringing Up Telephone Basics

Before you find out how to make a call, knowing a
little bit about the phone itself is helpful. In the following sections, we give you some basic vocabulary
related to phones and describe the different types of
phones and phone calls.

Brushing up on phone vocabulary

When somebody wants to talk to you, he may want
zvonit' (zvah-*neet';* to call) you. The caller needs
nabirat' (nuh-bee-*raht';* to dial) your **nomyer
tyelyefona** (*noh*-meer tee-lee-*foh*-nuh; telephone
number), and when the call goes through, you hear
a **zvonok** (zvah-*nohk;* ring). Here are some other
important words related to the **tyelyefon:**

✔ **byesprovodnoj tyelyefon** (bees-pruh-vahd-*nohy*
tee-lee-*fohn;* cordless phone)

✔ **diskovyj tyelyefon** (*dees*-kuh-vihy tee-lee-*fohn;*
rotary phone)

✔ **dolgij gudok** (*dohl*-geey goo-*dohk;* dial tone
[*literally:* long tone])

✔ **gudok** (goo-*dohk;* beep or tone)

✔ **knopka** (*knohp*-kuh; button)

✔ **knopochnyj tyelyefon** (*knoh*-puhch-nihy tee-lee-
fohn; touch-tone phone)

✔ **kod goroda** (kohd *goh*-ruh-duh; area code)

✔ **korotkiye gudki** (kah-*roht*-kee-ee goot-*kee;* busy
signal [*literally:* short tones])

✔ **mobil'nyj tyelyefon** (mah-*beel'*-nihy tee-lee-*fohn;* mobile phone)

✔ **myestnyj zvonok** (*myest*-nihy zvah-*nohk,* local call)

✔ **myezdugorodnyj zvonok** (myezh-doo-gah-*rohd*-nihy zvah-*nohk;* long-distance call [*literally:* intercity])

✔ **myezhdunarodnyj zvonok** (myezh-doo-nuh-*rohd*-nihy zvah-*nohk;* international call)

✔ **sotovyj tyelyefon** (*soh*-tuh-vihy tee-lee-*fohn;* cell phone)

✔ **tyelyefonnaya budka** (tee-lee-*fohn*-nuh-ye *boot*-kuh; telephone booth)

✔ **tyelyefonnaya kniga** (tee-lee-*fohn*-nuh-ye *knee*-guh; telephone book)

Russian makes a grammatical distinction between calling a person, calling an institution, and calling a different city or a country. The following rules apply. (See Chapter 2 for more details about cases.)

✔ If you're calling a person, use the dative case, as in **Ya khochu pozvonit' Natashye.** (ya khah-*choo* puh-zvah-*neet'* nuh-*tah*-shih; I want to call Natasha.)

✔ If you're calling an institution, after the verb, use the preposition **v** or **na** + the accusative case to indicate the institution you're calling, as in **zvonit' na rabotu** (zvah-*neet'* nuh ruh-*boh*-too; to call work) or **zvonit' v magazin** (zvah-*neet'* v muh-guh-*zeen;* to call a store).

✔ If you're calling a foreign country or another city, after the verb, use **v** + the accusative form of the city or country you're calling, as in **zvonit' v Amyeriku** (zvah-*neet'* v uh-*mye*-ree-koo; to call the United States).

Basic telephone etiquette

Every culture has its own telephone etiquette, and Russia is no exception.

When you make a phone call in Russia, the person who answers may say:

- ✔ **Alyo!** (uh-*lyo!;* Hello!)
- ✔ **Da.** (dah; Yes.)
- ✔ **Slushayu.** (*sloo*-shuh-yu; I'm listening.)

In English, you often say something like "Is John there?" Not so in Russian. In fact, a Russian may not even understand what you mean by that question. Instead, get to your request right away, using the phrase **Mozhno . . .** (*mohzh*-nuh . . . ; May I speak to . . .) + the name of the person you want to talk to. If you want to talk to a woman named **Natalya Ivanovna,** you say **Mozhno Natalyu Ivanovnu?** (*mohzh*-nuh nuh-*tahl'*-yu ee-*vah*-nuhv-noo?; May I speak to Natalya Ivanovna?)

Note that you have to use the name of the person you want to talk to in the accusative case. That's because what you're saying is an abbreviated **Mozhno pozvat' k tyelyefonu Natalyu Ivanovnu?** (*mohzh*-nuh pahz-*vaht'* k tee-lee-*foh*-noo nuh-*tahl'*-yu ee-*vah*-nuhv-noo?; Can you call to the phone Natalya Ivanovna?), and the verb **pozvat'** (pahz-*vaht';* to call) requires that the noun after it is used in the accusative case. (For more on the accusative case, see Chapter 2.) You can make this phrase more polite by adding the phrase **bud'tye dobry** (*bood'*-tee dahb-*rih;* will you be so kind) at the beginning.

Anticipating different responses

Here are some of the more common things you may hear in response after you ask for the person you want to speak to:

✔ If you call somebody at home and he or she is not at home, you most likely hear **Yego/yeyo nyet doma.** (ee-*voh*/*ee*-yo nyet *doh*-muh; He/she is not at home.)

✔ If the person you call is at home but he or she is not the one who answered the phone, you hear **Syejchas** (see-*chahs;* Hold on) or **Syejchas pozovu** (see-*chahs* puh-zah-*voo;* Hold on, I'll get him/her).

✔ When the person you want finally answers the phone (or if he or she actually picked up the phone when you called), he or she will say **Alyo** (uh-*lyo;* Hello) or **Slushayu** (*sloo*-shuh-yu; Speaking) or simply **Da** (dah; Yes).

✔ You probably have the wrong number if you hear **Kogo?** (kah-*voh;* Whom?) If the person knows you called the wrong number, you most likely will hear **Vy nye tuda popali.** (vih nee too-*dah* pah-*pah*-lee; You dialed the wrong number.)

You can also check to make sure you dialed the right number by saying something like **Eto pyat'sot dyevyanosto vosyem' sorok pyat' dvadtsat odin?** (*eh*-tuh peet-*soht* dee-vee-*nohs*-tuh *voh*-seem' *soh*-ruhk pyat' *dvaht*-tsuht' ah-*deen?;* Is this five nine eight four five two one? [*literally:* Is this five hundred ninety-eight forty-five twenty-one?]) If you dialed another number, you may hear **Nyet, vy nyepravil'no nabirayete.** (nyet vih nee-*prah*-veel'-nuh nuh-bee-*rah*-ee-tee; No, you've dialed the wrong number.)

Leaving a message with a person

If you call somebody and the person isn't available, you'll probably hear one of these phrases:

- ✔ **A kto yego/yeyo sprashivayet?** (uh ktoh yee-*voh*/yee-*yo* *sprah*-shih-vuh-eet?; And who is asking for him/her?)

- ✔ **A chto yemu pyeryedat'?** (uh shtoh yee-*moo* pee-ree-*daht'?;* Can I take a message? [if the person you're leaving a message for is a man].)

- ✔ **A chto yej pyeryedat'?** (uh shtoh yey pee-ree-*daht'?;* Can I take a message? [if the person you're leaving a message for is a woman].)

When you're asked who is calling, say: **Eto** (*eh*-tuh; This is . . . calling) + your name. Then you may simply want to give your phone number and say **Spasibo** (spuh-*see*-buh; thank you).

To ask to leave a message, begin your request with **A vy nye mozhyetye yemu/yey pyeryedat'?** (uh vih nee-*moh*-zhih-tee yee-*moo*/yey pee-ree-*daht'?;* Can I leave a message for him/her? [*literally:* please, tell him/her].)

No matter what your message is, it should begin with the phrase **Pyeryedajte pozhalujsta . . .** (pee-ree-*dahy*-tee pah-*zhah*-luh-stuh; Please tell him/her . . .) Most likely, you want to say

- ✔ **Pyeryedajte pozhalujsta chto zvonil** (pee-ree-*dahy*-tee pah-*zhah*-luh-stuh shtoh zvah-*neel;* Please tell him/her that . . . called) + your name (if you are a man).

- ✔ **Pyeryedajte pozhalujsta chto zvonila** (pee-ree-*dahy*-tee pah-*zhah*-luh-stuh shtoh zvah-*nee*-luh; Please tell him/her that . . . called) + your name (if you are a woman).

Words to Know

Vy nye znayetye gdye ona?	vih nee <u>znah</u>-ee-tee <u>gdye</u> ah-nah?	Do you happen to know where she is?
Kogda ona budyet doma?	kahg-<u>dah</u> ah-<u>nah</u><u>boo</u>-deet <u>doh</u>-muh?	When will she be home?
Ona dolzhna vyernut'sya . . .	ah-<u>nah</u> dahl-<u>zhnah</u> veer-<u>noot'</u>-sye . . .	She should be back . . .
Mozhyet byt' chto-nibud' pyeryedat'?	<u>moh</u>-zhit biht' <u>shtoh</u>-nee-boot' pee-ree-<u>daht</u>'?	Would you like to leave a message?
Ya pyeryezvonyu.	ya pee-reez-vah-nyu.	I'll call back.
Ya yej skazhu, chto ty zvonila.	ya yey skuh-zhoo shtoh tih zvah-nee-luh.	I will tell her that you called.

Talking to an answering machine

If you get an **avtootvyetchik** (uhf-tuh-aht-*vyet*-chee-keek; answering machine) the first thing you'll probably hear is **Zdravstvujte, k sozhaleniju, ja ne mogu otvetit' na Vash zvonok. Ostav'tye, pozhalujsta soobsh'yeniye poslye gudka.** (*zdrah*-stvooy-tee, k suh-zhuh-*lyeh*-nee-yoo, yah nee mah-*goo* aht-veh-teet' nuh vahsh zvah-nohk. ahs-*tahf*-tee, pah-*zhah-luh*-stuh suh-ahp-*sh'ye*-nee-eh *pohs*-lee goot-*kah;* Hello, unfortunately, I cannot take your call now. Please leave your message after the beep.)

On a cell phone voice mail, you're likely to hear a slightly different message from the one you hear on a regular answering machine: **Abonyent nye dostupyen. Ostav'tye soobsh'yeniye poslye signala.** (uh-bah-*nyent* nee dahs-*too*-peen ahs-*tahf*-tee suh-ahp-*sh'ye*-nee-ee *pohs*-lee seeg-*nah*-luh; The person you are calling is not available. Leave a message after the beep.)

When leaving a message, you can say something along these lines: **Zdravstvujtye. Eto** + your name. **Pozvonitye mnye pozhalujsta. Moj nomyer tyelyefona** + your phone number (*zdrah*-stvooy-tee. *eh*-tuh . . . puhz-vah-*nee*-tee mnye pah-*zhah*-luh-stuh. moy *noh*-meer tee-lee-*foh*-nuh . . . ; Hello! This is . . . Call me please. My phone number is . . .)

Sending a Letter, a Fax, or an E-Mail

Strange as it may seem today in the age of e-mail and cell phones, people still sometimes write and send **pis'ma** (*pees'*-muh; letters).

The imperfective verb **posylat'** (puh-sih-*laht'*; to send) and its perfective counterpart **poslat'** (pahs-*laht'*) have different patterns of conjugation. Although **posylat'** is a nice regular verb and **poslat'** has nothing special about it in the past tense, it has a peculiar pattern of conjugation in the future tense, shown in Table 8-1. (Check out Chapter 2 for more about verbs in general, including imperfective and perfective verbs.)

Table 8-1	Conjugation of Poslat' in the Future Tense	
Conjugation	*Pronunciation*	*Translation*
ya poshlyu	ya pahsh-*lyu*	I will send
ty poshlyosh'	tih pahsh-*lyosh'*	You will send (informal singular)

Conjugation	Pronunciation	Translation
on/ona poshlyot	ohn/ah-nah pahsh-*lyot*	He/she will send
my poshlyom	mih pahsh-*lyom*	We will send
vy poshlyotye	vih pah-*shlyo*-tee	You will send (formal singular and plural)
oni poshlyut	ah-*nee* pahsh-*lyut*	They will send

Just as in English, when sending written correspondence in Russian, it's customary to address the person you're writing to with the word *dear:*

- ✔ **uvazhajemyj** (oo-vah-*zhah*-yee-mihy; dear [masculine]) + the person's name

- ✔ **uvazhajemaja** (oo-vah-*zhah*-yee-muh-yuh; dear [feminine]) + the person's name

- ✔ **uvazhajemyje** (oo-vah-*zhah*-ye-mih-ye; dear [plural]) + the people's names

In more-formal situations, you should also include the date in the upper left-hand corner.

> The close of your letter may include the standard **vash** (vahsh; yours [formal]) or **tvoj** (tvohy; yours [informal]) plus your name. Or you use one of the following phrases, depending on your intention and your relationship to the recipient:

- ✔ **s uvazheniyem** (s oo-vuh-*zheh*-nee-eem; respectfully)

- ✔ **s lyubov'yu** (s lyu-*bohv'*-yoo; with love)

- ✔ **tseluyu** (tsih-*loo*-yoo; love [*literally:* I kiss you])

When you talk about **imyeil** (ee-*meh*-eel; e-mail) and **faks** (fahks; fax), use the same verb pair of **posylat'** and **poslat'** (to send) as you do when you talk about letters. For example, suppose you want to promise a client that you'll send him an e-mail; you simply say

Ya poshlyu tyebye imejl. (ya pahsh-*lyoo* tee-*bye* ee-*meh*-eel; I'll e-mail you.) If you promise to send him a fax, you say **Ya poshlyu tyebye faks.** (ya pahsh-*lyoo* tee-*bye* fahks; I'll send you a fax.) You also use the same verb pair when you attach documents to your e-mail. **Vlozhyennyj fajl/document** (*vloh*-zhyeh-nihy fahyl/duh-koo-*myent; literally:* an enclosed file/ document) or **prikryeplyonnij fajl/document** (pree-krye-*plyo*-nihy fahyl/duh-koo-*myent;* an attached file/document) are the two terms used most com- monly to refer to an e-mail attachment.

If you want to ask somebody what his or her e-mail address is, just say **Kakoj u vas imyeil?** (kuh-*kohy* oo vahs ee-*meh*-eel?; What is your e-mail address? [*literally:* What is your e-mail?]) But before you ask this question, you may want to make sure that this person has an e-mail account by asking **U vas yest' imyeil?** (oo vas yest' ee-*meh*-eel?; Do you have e-mail?)

Other words and expressions associated with corre- spondence include

- ✔ **nomyer faksa** (*noh*-meer *fahk*-suh; fax number)
- ✔ **pis'mo** (pees'-*moh;* letter)
- ✔ **pochta** (*pohch*-tuh; post office)
- ✔ **pochtovyj yash'ik** (pahch-*toh*-vihy *ya*-sh'eek; mailbox)
- ✔ **proverit' pochtu** (prah-*vyeh*-reet' *pohch*-too; to check your e-mail) or **prochitat' pochtu** (pruh- chee-*taht' pohch*-too; to read e-mails)

Chapter 9

I Get Around: Transportation

....

In This Chapter

▶ Moving along with motion verbs

▶ Making your way through the airport

▶ Exploring public transportation

▶ Asking directions

....

A s the Russian proverb has it, **Yazyk do Kiyeva dovyedyot** (ee-*zihk* dah *kee*-ee-vuh duh-vee-*dyot*), which translates as "Your tongue will lead you to Kiev," and basically means, "Ask questions, and you'll get anywhere." This chapter gives you all the phrases you need to navigate your way through the transportation maze.

Understanding Verbs of Motion

Every language has a lot of words for things the speakers of that language know well. That's why the Eskimos have 12 different words for *snow*. Russians have a lot of space to move around — maybe that's why they have so many different verbs of motion.

Your choice of verb depends on many different factors and your intended message. To mention just a few factors, the choice depends on

✔ Whether the motion is performed with a vehicle or without it

✔ Whether the motion indicates a regular habitual motion

✔ Whether the motion takes place at the moment of speaking

Going by foot or vehicle habitually

To indicate regular habitual motion in the present tense, you use the *multidirectional verbs* **khodit'** (khah-*deet'*; to go on foot) and **yezdit'** (*yez*-deet'; to go by vehicle). Think of places that you go to once a week, every day, two times a month, once a year, or every weekend. Most folks, for example, have to go to work every day. In Russian you say:

✔ **Ya khozhu na rabotu kazhdyj dyen'** (ya khah-*zhoo* nuh ruh-*boh*-too *kahzh*-dihy dyen'; I go to work every day) if you go by foot. (The verb **khodit'** is conjugated in Table 9-1.)

✔ **Ya yezzhu na rabotu kazhdyj dyen'** (ya *yez*-zhoo nuh ruh-*boh*-too *kahzh*-dihy dyen'; I go to work every day) if you go by vehicle. (The verb **yezdit'** is conjugated in Table 9-2.)

 When you talk about walking, you also can use the expression **khodit' pyeshkom** (khah-*deet'* peesh-*kohm;* to go by foot, to walk). This expression sounds redundant, but that's the way it's used in Russian.

Table 9-1	Conjugation of Khodit'	
Conjugation	*Pronunciation*	*Translation*
ya khozhu	ya khah-*zhoo*	I go on foot
ty khodish'	tih *khoh*-deesh'	You go on foot (informal singular)

Conjugation	Pronunciation	Translation
on/ona/ono khodit	ohn/oh-*nah*/ah-*noh* khoh-deet	He/she/it goes on foot
my khodim	mih *khoh*-deem	We go on foot
vy khoditye	vih *khoh*-dee-tee	You go on foot (formal singular; plural)
oni khodyat	ah-*nee khoh*-dyet	They go on foot

Table 9-2	Conjugation of Yezdit'	
Conjugation	Pronunciation	Translation
ya yezzhu	ya *yez*-zhoo	I go by vehicle
ty yezdish'	tih *yez*-deesh'	You go by vehicle (informal singular)
on/ona/ono yezdit	ohn/ah-*nah*/ah-*noh yez*-deet	He/she/it goes by vehicle
my yezdim	mih *yez*-deem	We go by vehicle
vy yezdite	vih *yez*-dee-tee	You go by vehicle (formal singular; plural)
oni yezdyat	ah-*nee yez*-dyet	They go by vehicle

You also can specify the vehicle you're using with one of these phrases:

- **yezdit' na avtobusye** (*yez*-deet' nah uhf-*toh*-boo-see; to go by bus)
- **yezdit' na marshrutkye** (*yez*-deet' nah muhr-*shroot*-kee; to go by minivan)
- **yezdit' na mashinye** (yiez-deet' nah muh-*shih*-nee; to go by car)

> ✔ **yezdit' na myetro** (*yez*-deet' nah mee-*troh*; to go
> by metro)

> ✔ **yezdit' na poyezdye** (*yez*-deet' nah *noh*-yeez-dee;
> to go by train)

> ✔ **yezdit' na taksi** (*yez*-deet' nah tuhk-*see*; to go
> by taxi)

Going by foot or vehicle at the present time

You use different verbs (called *unidirectional verbs*) to
specify that you're moving in a specific direction or to
a specific place. You also use these verbs to indicate
motion performed at the present moment.

For walking, use the verb **idti** (ee-*tee;* to go in one
direction by foot), such as in the phrase **Ya idu na
rabotu** (ya ee-*doo* nuh ruh-*boh*-too; I am walking to
work). The verb **idti** is conjugated in Table 9-3.

Table 9-3	Conjugation of Idti	
Conjugation	*Pronunciation*	*Translation*
ya idu	yah ee-*doo*	I am going
ty idyosh'	tih ee-*dyohsh'*	You are going (informal singular)
on/ona/ono idyot	ohn/ah-*nah*/ah-*noh* ee-*dyot*	He/she/it is going
my idyom	mih ee-*dyom*	We are going
vy idyotye	vih ee-*dyo*-tee	You are going (formal singular; plural)
oni idut	ah-*nee* ee-*doot*	They are going

For moving by a vehicle, use the unidirectional verb
yekhat' (*ye*-khaht'; to go in one direction by a vehicle). The verb **yekhat'** is conjugated in Table 9-4.

Table 9-4	Conjugation of Yekhat'	
Conjugation	Pronunciation	Translation
ya yedu	yah *ye*-doo	I am going
ty yedyesh'	tih *ye*-deesh'	You are going (informal singular)
on/ona/ono yedyet	ohn/ah-*nah*/ah-*noh* *ye*-deet	He/she/it is going
my yedyem	mih *ye*-deem	We are going
vy yedyetye	vih *ye*-dee-tee	You are going (formal singular; plural)
oni yedut	ah-*nee ye*-doot	They are going

Explaining where you're going

To tell where you're going specifically, use the prepositions **v** (v; to) or **na** (nah; to) + the accusative case of the place you're going:

> ✔ **Ya idu v tyeatr.** (ya ee-*doo* f tee-*ahtr;* I am going to the theater.)

> ✔ **Ona idyot na kontsyert.** (ah-*nah* ee-*dyot* nuh kahn-*tsehrt;* She is going to the concert.)

For walking or driving around a place, use the preposition **po** (pah; around) + the dative case. (For more information on cases, see Chapter 2.)

> ✔ **Ona khodit po Moskvye.** (ah-*nah* khoh-deet puh mahsk-*vye;* She walks around Moscow.)

> ✔ **My yezdim po tsyentru goroda.** (mih *yez*-deem pah *tsehnt*-roo *goh*-ruh-duh; We drive around downtown.)

Remember to use **yezdit'** or **yekhat'** (to go by vehicle) when you talk about going to other cities! Otherwise, if you say **ya idu v Moskvu** (ya ee-*doo* v mahsk-*voo*), you make it sound as though you're embarking on an enduring walking pilgrimage to Moscow, which is probably not your intention.

Navigating the Airport

The vocabulary in this section helps you plan and enjoy your trip by **samolyot** (suh-mah-*lyot;* plane).

You use a special verb of motion when you talk about flying: **lyetyet'** (lee-*tyet';* to fly). You can't use the verb **yekhat'** when you talk about traveling by plane, unless the plane is wheeling around the airport without actually leaving the ground. If the plane actually takes off, you have to use the verb **lyetyet'.**

Checking in and boarding your flight

When you arrive at the **aeroport** (ah-eh-rah-*pohrt;* airport), the following words will help you navigate:

- ✔ **bilyet** (bee-*lyet;* ticket)
- ✔ **informatsionnoye tablo** (een-fuhr-muh-tsih-*oh*-nuh-ye tahb-*loh;* departures and arrivals display)
- ✔ **myesto u okna** (*myes*-tuh oo ahk-*nah;* window seat)
- ✔ **myesto u prokhoda** (*myes*-tuh oo prah-*khoh*-duh; aisle seat)
- ✔ **myetalloiskatyel'** (mee-*tah*-luh-ees-*kah*-teel'; metal detector)
- ✔ **nomyer ryejsa** (*noh*-meer *ryey*-suh; flight number)
- ✔ **otpravlyeniye** (uht-pruhv-*lye*-nee-eh; departures)
- ✔ **pasport** (*pahs*-puhrt; passport)
- ✔ **posadochnyj talon** (pah-*sah*-duhch-nihy tuh-*lohn;* boarding pass)
- ✔ **pribytiye** (pree-*bih*-tee-eh; arrivals)

- ✔ **ruchnoj bagazh** (rooch-*nohy* buh-*gahsh;* carryon)

- ✔ **ryegistratsiya** (ree-geest-*rah*-tsih-ye; check-in)

- ✔ **sluzhba byezopasnosti** (*sloozh*-buh bee-zah-*pahs*-nuhs-tee; security service)

Here are some questions you may hear or ask as you check in:

- ✔ **Vy budyetye sdavat' bagazh?** (vih *boo*-dee-tee zdah-*vaht'* buh-*gahsh?;* Are you checking any luggage?)

- ✔ **Vy ostavlyali vash bagazh byez prismotra?** (vih ahs-tahv-*lya*-lee vahsh buh-*gahsh* byes pree-*smoh*-truh?; Have you left your luggage unattended?)

- ✔ **Kakoj u myenya nomyer vykhoda?** (kuh-*kohy* oo mee-*nya noh*-meer *vih*-khuh-duh?; What's my gate number?)

- ✔ **Eto ryejs v . . . ?** (*eh*-tuh ryeys v . . . ?; Is this the flight to . . . ?)

Handling passport control and Customs

After leaving the plane and walking through a corridor maze, you see a crowded hall with **pasportnyj kontrol'** (*pahs*-puhrt-nihy kahnt-*rohl';* passport control). Make sure you get into the right line: One line is for **grazhdanye Rossii** (*grahzh*-duh-nee rah-*see*-ee; Russian citizens), and one is for **inostranniye grazhdanye** (ee-nahs-*trah*-nih-ee *grahzh*-duh-nee; foreign citizens).

At passport control, you show your **pasport** (*pahs*-puhrt; passport) and **viza** (*vee*-zah; visa). A **pogranichnik** (puhg-ruh-*neech*-neek; border official) asks you **Tsyel' priyezda?** (tsehl' pree-*yez*-duh; The purpose of your visit?) You may answer:

- ✔ **chastnyj vizit** (*chahs*-nihy vee-*zeet*; private visit)

- ✔ **rabota** (ruh-*boh*-tuh; work)

- ✔ **turizm** (too-*reezm*; tourism)

- ✔ **uchyoba** (oo-*choh*-buh; studies)

After you pick up your **bagazh,** the next step is going through **tamozhyennyj dosmotr** (tuh-*moh*-zhih-nihy dahs-*mohtr;* Customs). The best way to go is **zyelyonyj koridor** (zee-*lyo*-nihy kuh-ree-*dohr;* nothing to declare passage way [*literally:* green corridor]). Otherwise, you have to deal with **tamozhyenniki** (tuh-*moh*-zhih-nee-kee; Customs officers) and answer the question **Chto dyeklariruyete?** (shtoh deek-luh-*ree*-roo-ee-tee; What would you like to declare?)

To answer, say **Ya dyeklariruyu . . .** (ya deek-luh-*ree*-roo-yu; I'm declaring . . .) + the word for what you are declaring in the accusative case. The following items usually need to be declared:

- ✔ **alkogol'** (uhl-kah-*gohl';* alcohol)

- ✔ **dragotsyennosti** (druh-gah-*tseh*-nuhs-tee; jewelry)

- ✔ **proizvyedyeniya iskusstva** (pruh-eez-vee-*dye*-nee-ye ees-*koost*-vuh; works of art)

Conquering Public Transportation

Russians hop around their humongous cities with butterfly ease, changing two to three means of public transportation during a one-way trip to work. And so can you. You just need to know where to look for the information and how to ask the right questions, which you discover in the following sections.

Taking a taxi

When you call the **sluzhba taksi** (*sloozh*-buh tuhk-*see;* cab service), they ask:

- ✔ **vash adryes** (vahsh *ahd*-rees; your address)

- ✔ **Kuda yedyetye?** (koo-*dah* ye-dee-tee; Where are you going?)

You use **kuda** (koo-*dah;* where to) rather than **gdye** (gdye; where) when you're asking about movement toward a destination. You can think of **kuda** as meaning "Where to?" and **gdye** as simply "Where?" Likewise, you use **tuda** (too-*dah;* to there) instead of **tam** (tahm; there) when you want to emphasize movement toward a destination. Simply stated: With verbs of motion, you usually use **kuda** rather than **gdye,** and **tuda** rather than **tam.**

You can ask for your fare while you're ordering your cab: **Skol'ko eto budyet stoit'?** (*skohl'*-kuh *eh*-tuh *boo*-deet *stoh*-eet'?; How much would that be?) This fare is usually nonnegotiable. If you hail a cab in the street, however, you have plenty of room for negotiating.

You don't need **davat' chayevye** (duh-*vaht'* chee-ee-*vih*-ee; to give a tip) to cab drivers in Russia.

Using minivans

The transport of choice in today's Russia is the **marshrutka** (muhr-*shroot*-kuh), a minivan with a set route. **Marshrutki** (muhr-*shroot*-kee; minivans) are usually fast and often go to any destination. They stop only where passengers need to get off, so make sure you tell the driver something like **Ostanovitye, pozhalujsta, u vokzala?** (uh-stuh-nah-*vee*-tee pah-*zhah*-luh-stuh oo vahk-*zah*-luh?; Would you please stop at the railway station?)

Marshrutki have different routes, marked by numbers. You can recognize a **marshrutka** by a piece of paper with its number in the front window. To board a **marshrutka,** you need to go to a place where it stops. These places aren't usually marked, so you need to ask a local **Gdye ostanavlivayutsya marshrutki?** (gdye uhs-tuh-*nahv*-lee-vuh-yut-sye muhr-*shroot*-kee?; Where do the minivans stop?)

Catching buses, trolley buses, and trams

The first difficulty with all this variety of Russian public transportation is that, in English, all these things are called "buses." Here's a short comprehensive guide on how to tell one item from another:

- ✔ **avtobus** (uhf-*toh*-boos): A bus as you know it
- ✔ **trollyejbus** (trah-*lyey*-boos): A bus connected to electric wires above
- ✔ **tramvaj** (truhm-*vahy*): A bus connected to electric wires and running on rails

Unless you're into orienteering, the best way to find your route is to ask the locals. Just ask these questions:

- ✔ **Kak mnye doyekhat' do Krasnoj Plosh'adi?** (kahk mnye dah-*ye*-khuht' dah *krahs*-nuhy *ploh*-sh'ee-dee?; How can I get to the Red Square?)
- ✔ **Etot avtobus idyot do Ermitazha?** (*eh*-tuht uhf-*toh*-boos ee-*dyot* duh ehr-mee-*tah*-zhuh?; Will this bus take me to the Hermitage?)
- ✔ **Gdye mozhno kupit' bilyety?** (gdye *mohzh*-nuh koo-*peet'* bee-*lye*-tih?; Where can I buy tickets?)

Ways to pay for a bus ride vary. In some cities, you need to buy **bilyety** (bee-*lye*-tih; tickets) ahead of time in **kioski** (kee-*ohs*-kee; ticket kiosks). In others, you pay directly to the **vodityel'** (vah-*dee*-teel'; driver) or **konduktor** (kahn-*dook*-tuhr; bus conductor) when you board the bus.

Hopping onto the subway

The Russian **myetro** (mee-*troh;* subway) is beautiful, clean, user-friendly, and cheap. It connects the most distant parts of such humongous cities as Moscow, and it's impenetrable to traffic complications. During the day, trains come every two to three minutes. Unfortunately, it's usually closed between 1:30 a.m.

and 4:30 a.m. Around 4:30 a.m., you can easily locate a **stantsiya myetro** (*stahn*-tsee-ye meet-*roh;* subway sta-tion) on a Moscow street by a crowd of young people in clubbing clothes waiting for the **myetro** to open so they can go home.

To take the **myetro,** you need to buy a **kartochka** (*kahr*-tuhch-kuh; fare card) for any number of trips or a **proyezdnoj** (pruh-eez-*nohy;* pass). Both are available in the **vyestibyul' myetro** (vees-tee-*byul* meet-*roh;* metro foyer).

Hopping on a train

Trains are a great way to travel. The types of trains, in the order of increasing price and quality, are

- ✔ **elyektrichka** (eh-leek-*treech*-kuh; a suburban train)
- ✔ **skorostnoj poyezd** (skuh-rahs-*nohy* poh-ehst; a low-speed train)
- ✔ **skoryj poyezd** (*skoh*-rihy poh-ehst; a faster and more expensive train)
- ✔ **firmyennyj poyezd** (*feer*-mee-nihy poh-eehst; a premium train [*literally:* company train])

You can **kupit' bilyety** (koo-*peet'* bee-*lye*-tih; buy tick-ets) directly at the railway station, at a travel agency, or in a **zhyelyeznodorozhnyye kassy** (zhih-*lyez*-nuh-dah-*rohzh*-nih-ee *kah*-sih; railway ticket office).

You can start your dialogue with **Mnye nuzhyen bilyet v** (mnye *noo*-zheen bee-*lyet* v; I need a ticket to) + the name of the city you're heading for, in the accusative case (see Chapter 2 for more on cases). The ticket salesperson will probably ask you the fol-lowing questions:

- ✔ **Na kakoye chislo?** (nuh kuh-*koh*-eh chees-*loh?;* For what date?)
- ✔ **Vam kupye ili platskart?** (vahm koo-*peh ee*-lee pluhts-*kahrt?;* Would you like a compartment car or a reserved berth?)

> ✔ **V odnu storonu ili tuda i obratno?** (v ahd-*noo* *stoh*-ruh-noo *ee*-lee too-*dah* ee ah-*braht*-nuh?; One way or round trip?)

You can also tell the ticket salesperson what kind of seat you prefer: **vyerkhnyaya polka** (*vyerkh*-nee-ye *pohl*-kuh; top fold-down bed) or **nizhnyaya polka** (*neezh*-nye-ye *pohl*-kuh; bottom fold-down bed). On **elyektrichki** (eh-leek-*treech*-kee; suburban trains), which don't have fold-down beds, seats aren't assigned.

Asking "Where" and "How" Questions

When in doubt, just ask! In the following sections you discover how to ask for directions with two simple words: *where* and *how*.

Where is it?

 Russian uses two words to translate the English *where* — **gdye** (gdye; where) or **kuda** (koo-*dah*; where). But you can't use the two words interchangeably. The following is what you need to know about these words:

> ✔ If "where" indicates *location* rather than direction of movement and you aren't using the so-called verbs of motion (to go, to walk, to drive, and so on), use the word **gdye** (where).

> ✔ If "where" indicates *direction* of movement rather than location, or in other words is used in a sentence with verbs of motion (to go, to walk, to drive, and so on), use the word **kuda** (where).

So if you're inquiring about location or destination you can ask:

Gdye blizhayshaya ostanovka avtobusa? (gdye blee-*zhahy*-shuh-ye uhs-tuh-*nohf*-kuh uhf-toh-boo-suh?; Where is the nearest bus stop?)

Gdye bibliotyeka? (gdye beeb-lee-ah-*tye*-kuh?; Where is the library?)

But if you're asking about direction, you ask:

Kuda idyot etot avtobus? (koo-*dah* ee-*dyot* eh-tuht uhf-*toh*-boos?; Where is this bus going?)

How do I get there?

To ask how to get somewhere — say, the **muzyyej** (moo-*zyey;* museum) — you need the verb **popast'** (pah-*pahst';* to get to). This verb, too, belongs to the category of verbs of motion.

Kak ya otsyuda mogu popast' v muzyej? (kahk ya aht-*syu*-duh mah-*goo* pah-*pahst'* v moo-*zyey?;* How do I get to the museum from here?)

Or you may want to make your question more impersonal by saying **Kak otsyuda mozhno popast' v** (How does one get to . . . ?):

Kak otsyuda mozhno popast' v muzyej? (kaht aht-*syu*-duh *mohzh*-nuh pah-*pahst'* v moo-*zyey?;* How does one get to the museum from here?)

Understanding Specific Directions

When you're done asking for directions, you need to understand what you're being told. In the following sections, you find out about prepositions and other words people use when talking about directions in Russian.

Recognizing prepositions

Russian uses the same prepositions, v/na, to express both "to (a place)" and "in/at (a place)." When you use **v/na** to indicate movement, the noun indicating the place of destination takes the accusative case. If **v/na** is used to denote location, the noun denoting location is used in prepositional case. Compare these two sentences:

> ✔ **Ya idu v bibliotyeku.** (ya ee-*doo* v beeb-lee-ah-*tye*-koo; I am going to the library.)

> ✔ **Ya v bibliotyekye.** (ya v beeb-lee-ah-*tye*-kee; I am at the library.)

So when do you use **na** and when do you use **v?** The choice of the preposition depends on the noun it's used with. With most nouns, Russian speakers use **v.** But a number of nouns, such as those in the following list, require **na** (you just need to remember them).

> ✔ **na lyektsiyu/na lyektsii** (nuh *lyek*-tsih-yu/nuh *lyek*-tsih-ee; to a lecture/at a lecture)

> ✔ **na stantsiyu/na stantsii** (nuh *stahn*-tsih-yu/nuh *stahn*-tsih-ee; to a station/at a station)

> ✔ **na urok/na urokye** (nuh oo-*rohk*/nuh oo-*roh*-kee; to a class/at a class)

> ✔ **na vokzal/na vokzalye** (nuh vahk-*zahl*/nuh vahk-*zah*-lee; to a railway station/at a railway station)

Some other prepositions that are helpful in directions are:

> ✔ **okolo** (*oh*-kuh-luh; near) + a noun in the genitive case

> ✔ **ryadom s** (*rya*-duhm s; next to) + a noun in the instrumental case

- ✔ **naprotiv** (nuh-*proh*-teef; opposite, across from) + a noun in the genitive case
- ✔ **za** (zah; behind, beyond) + a noun in the instrumental case
- ✔ **pozadi** (puh-zuh-*dee;* behind) + a noun in the genitive case
- ✔ **pyered** (*pye*-reet; in front of) + a noun in the instrumental case
- ✔ **myezhdu** (*myezh*-doo; between) + a noun in the instrumental case
- ✔ **vnutri** (vnoo-*tree;* inside) + a noun in the genitive case
- ✔ **snaruzhi** (snuh-*roo*-zhih; outside) + a noun in the genitive case
- ✔ **nad** (naht; above) + a noun in the instrumental case
- ✔ **pod** (poht; below) + a noun in the instrumental case

Keeping "right" and "left" straight

When people give you directions, they also often use these words:

- ✔ **sprava ot** (*sprah*-vuh uht; to the right of) + a noun in the genitive case
- ✔ **napravo** (nuh-*prah*-vuh; to the right)
- ✔ **slyeva ot** (*slye*-vuh uht; to the left of) + a noun in the genitive case
- ✔ **nalyevo** (nuh-*lye*-vuh; to the left)
- ✔ **na lyevoj storonye** (nuh *lye*-vuhy stuh-rah-*nye;* on the left side)
- ✔ **na pravoj storonye** (nuh *prah*-vahy stuh-rah-*nye;* on the right side)

Here's a short exchange that may take place between you and a friendly-looking Russian woman:

> **You: Izvinitye, gdye magazin?** (eez-vee-*nee*-tee gdye muh-guh-*zeen?;* Excuse me, where is the store?)

> The woman: **Magazin sprava ot aptyeki.** (muh-guh-*zeen sprah*-vuh uht uhp-*tye*-kee; The store is to the right of the pharmacy.)

Making sense of commands

Here are some useful phrases in the imperative mood you may hear or want to use when giving directions:

- ✔ **Iditye praymo.** (ee-*dee*-tee *prya*-muh; Go straight.)

- ✔ **Iditye nazad.** (ee-*dee*-tee nuh-*zaht;* Go back.)

- ✔ **Iditye pryamo do . . .** (ee-*dee*-tee *prya*-muh duh; Go as far as . . .) + the noun in the genitive case

- ✔ **Podojditye k . . .** (puh-duhy-*dee*-tee k; Go up to . . .) + the noun in the dative case

- ✔ **Iditye po . . .** (ee-*dee*-tee puh; Go down along . . .) + the noun in the dative case

- ✔ **Iditye mimo . . .** (ee-*dee*-tee *mee*-muh; Pass by . . .) + the noun in the genitive case

- ✔ **Povyernitye nalyevo!** (puh-veer-*nee*-tee nuh-*lye*-vuh; Turn left or take a left turn.)

- ✔ **Povyernitye napravo!** (puh-veer-*nee*-tee nuh-*prah*-vuh; Turn right or take a right turn.)

- ✔ **Zavyernitye za ugol!** (zuh-veer-*nee*-tee *zah*-oo-guhl; Turn around the corner.)

- ✔ **Pyeryejditye ulitsu!** (pee-reey-*dee*-tee oo-leet-soo; Cross the street.)

- ✔ **Pyeryejditye plosh'ad'!** (pee-reey-*dee*-tee *ploh*-sh'uht'; Cross the square.)

- ✔ **Pyeryejditye chyerez dorogu!** (pee-reey-*dee*-tee *cheh*-reez dah-*roh*-goo; Cross the street/road.)

To form the imperative when you're talking to somebody with whom you're on **vy** (vih; you [formal singular; plural]) terms, such as strangers, add **–tye** as we did in the previous list. When you're speaking to somebody with whom you're on **ty** (tih; you [informal singular]) terms, you can remove the **–tye.** For example, to say "Turn left" to a friend, you say **Povyerni nalyevo.** (puh-veer-*nee* nuh-*lye*-vuh; Turn left.)

Curiously enough, Russians don't like to indicate directions with the words **vostok** (vahs-*tohk*; east), **zapad** (*zah*-puht; west), **syever** (*sye*-veer; north), and **yug** (yuk; south). They seem to avoid them when explaining how you can reach your place of destination. Phrases like *Go south, Turn west,* and *Drive south* are very rare in direction-giving.

Words to Know

Kak mnye otsyuda popast' v . . .	kahk mnye aht-<u>syu</u>-duh pah-<u>pahst'</u> v . . .	How can I get to . . . from here?
nakhoditsya	nuh-<u>khoh</u>-deet-sye	is located
vyjti na	<u>vihy</u>-tee nuh	go out to
Nikuda nye svorachivaya	nee-koo-<u>dah</u> nee svah-<u>rah</u>-chee-vuh-ye	Without turning anywhere
Kogda dojdyotye do . . .	kahg-<u>dah</u> dahy-<u>dyo</u>-tee duh . . .	When you reach . . .
opyat'	ah-<u>pyat'</u>	again
na uglu	nuh oog-<u>loo</u>	on the corner

Describing Distances

Sometimes you don't want detailed information about directions. You just want to know whether someplace is near or far and how long it takes to get there. Here are some helpful phrases:

✔ **Eto dalyeko?** (*eh*-tuh duh-lee-*koh?;* Is it far away?)

✔ **Eto dovol'no dalyeko. Dvye ostanovki na tramvaye/avtobusye/trolyejbusye/myetro.** (*eh*-tuh dah-*vohl'*-nuh duh-lee-*koh*. dvye uhs-tuh-*nohf*-kee nuh truhm-*vahy*-ee/uhf-*toh*-boo-see/trah-*lyey*-boo-see/meet-*roh;* That's quite far away. Two stops by the tram/bus/trolleybus/metro.)

✔ **Eto nedalyeko. Minut pyatnadtsat' pyeshkom.** (*eh*-tuh nee-duh-lee-*koh*. mee-*noot* peet-*naht*-suht peesh-*kohm;* It's not far away. About fifteen minutes' walk.)

You may notice that in both the previous responses, the word **minut** (minutes) is placed before the numeral **pyatnadtsat'** (fifteen), and you may be wondering whether it's an error. Nope, that's not an error! Russian has a very special way of indicating approximate time, weight, distance, or even prices. Where English uses the word *about,* Russian may simply use the method of reversing the order of words, as in **Minut pyatnadtsat' pyeshkom** (mee-*noot* peet-*naht*-suht' peesh-*kohm;* About fifteen minutes' walk). To be more exact, a Russian would say **Pyatnadtsat' minut pyeshkom** (peet-*naht*-suht' mee-*noot* peesh-*kohm;* Exactly fifteen minutes' walk).

Chapter 10

Laying Down Your Weary Head: House or Hotel

• •

In This Chapter

▶ Locating an apartment

▶ Finding the hotel of your dreams

▶ Checking in and checking out

• •

*W*hether you've been working at the office, shopping, or traveling, at the end of the day, you need a place to lay your head. This chapter gives you the phrases you need to get around your house or to find a hotel.

Hunting for an Apartment or a House

Finding an apartment or a house is stressful enough in English. Are you looking for a good view or a central location? What's more important: a big kitchen or hardwood floors? And how squeaky are those hardwood floors? Equip yourself with phrases introduced in the following sections, and good luck in your hunt for a home!

Talking about an apartment or a house

A Russian **kvartira** (kvuhr-*tee*-ruh; apartment) is generally small. For example, **odnokomnatnaya** (uhd-nah-*kohm*-nuht-nuh-yuh) **kvartira** literally means one-room apartment. It has, literally, one room and a kitchen (which is usually used as a dining room, no matter how tiny it is). So, a more accurate equivalent for a Russian **odnokomnatnaya kvartira** is "a studio apartment."

If you like to live large, you may want to look at a **dvukhkomnatnaya kvartira** (dvookh-*kohm*-nuht-nuh-yuh kvuhr-*tee*-ruh; two-room apartment) or even a **tryokhkomnatnaya kvartira** (tryokh-*kohm*-nuht-nuh-yuh kvuhr-*tee*-ruh; three-room apartment).

Here are some other phrases you use and hear when talking about an apartment:

- ✔ **kvartira na pyervom etazhye** (kvuhr-*tee*-ruh nuh *pyer*-vuhm eh-tuh-*zheh*; a first-floor apartment)

- ✔ **kvartira na vtorom etazhye** (kvuhr-*tee*-ruh nuh ftah-*rohm* eh-tuh-*zheh*; a second-floor apartment)

- ✔ **kvartira s myebyel'yu** (kvuhr-*tee*-ruh s *m'eh*-bee-l'yu; furnished apartment)

- ✔ **sdat' kvartiru** (zdaht' kvuhr-*tee*-roo; to rent out an apartment)

- ✔ **snyat' kvartiru** (sn'aht' kvuhr-*tee*-roo; to rent an apartment)

Although Russians do use the word **ryenta** (*r'ehn*-tuh; rent), it isn't usually used to talk about private apartments. To inquire about the price of an apartment, ask about **plata za kvartiru** (*plah*-tuh zuh kvuhr-*tee*-roo; payment for the apartment) or **stoimost' prozhivaniya v myesyats** (*stoh*-ee-muhst'

pruh-zhih-*vah*-nee-uh v *mye*-seets; cost of
living per month). When you make your payments, use the expression **platit' za kvartiru**
(pluh-*teet'* zuh kvuhr-*tee*-roo; pay for the
apartment).

If you're looking in the newspaper for apartments, look
for the **Ob'yavleniya** (ahb'-yeev-l'*eh*-nee-uh; classi-
fieds) section. You have several ways to say "apartments for rent" in Russian. Any of the following is
likely to pop up in the newspaper you're looking at:

✔ **aryenda kvartir** (uh-r'*ehn*-duh kvuhr-*teer*; rent
of apartments)

✔ **kvartiry v nayom** (kvuhr-*tee*-rih v nuh-*yom*;
apartments to rent)

✔ **sdayu** (sduh-*yoo*; I am renting out)

✔ **snyat' zhil'yo** (sn'aht' zhihl'-*yo*; to rent a place)

The ads you find are probably saturated with
abbreviations such as **kmn** for **komnata**
(*kohm*-nuh-tuh; room) and **m.** for **metro** or
stantsiya myetro (stahn-tsih-yuh meet-*roh*;
subway station). Because the metro is such a
prominent means of getting around, Russians
use names of metro stations to describe location. Thus, if the ad says **m. Tverskaya,** the
apartment is located next to metro station
Tverskaya — in downtown Moscow!

Your ad may also say **nye agenstvo** (nee uh-*g'ehn*-
stvuh; not an agency). What this means is that the ad
was posted by the landlord himself, which allows him
to cut the cost of a rental-agency fee.

The rules for finding a **dom** (dohm; house) are pretty
much the same as those for finding an apartment.
You can check out newspaper ads about selling
nyedvizhimost' (need-*vee*-zhih-muhst'; real estate)
or talk to an **agyent po prodazhye nyedvizhimosti**
(uh-*g'ehnt* puh prah-*dah*-zhih need-*vee*-zhih-muhs-tee;
real estate agent).

Asking the right questions

Some questions you definitely want to ask your **agyent po s'yomu zhil'ya** (uh-g'ehnt pah s'yo-moo zhih-l'ya; real estate agent) or **khozyain/khozyajka** (khah-z'ah-een/khah-z'ah-koo; landlord/landlady):

- ✔ **Mnye nuzhno platit' dyeposit?** (mn'eh noozh-nuh plah-teet' dee-pah-zeet?; Do I need to pay the deposit?)

- ✔ **Kto platit za uslugi — elyektrichyestvo, gaz, vodu?** (ktoh plah-teet zuh oos-loo-gee — eh-leek-tree-chees-tvuh, gahs, voh-doo?; Who pays for utilities — electricity, gas, water?)

- ✔ **Kakaya oplata v myesyats?** (kuh-kah-yuh ahp-lah-tuh v m'eh-seets?; What are the monthly payments?)

- ✔ **Vy khotitye, chtoby ya platil rublyami ili dollarami?** (vih khah-tee-tee shtoh-bih ya pluh-teel roob-l'ah-mee ee-lee doh-luh-ruh-mee?; Do you want me to pay in rubles or in dollars?)

- ✔ **Eto spokojnyj rayon?** (eh-tuh spah-kohy-nihy ruh-yon?; Is it a safe neighborhood?)

- ✔ **Kto zanimayetsya pochinkoj nyeispravnostyej?** (ktoh zuh-nee-mah-ee-tsuh pah-cheen-kuhy nee-ees-prahv-nuhs-t'ehy?; Who performs the maintenance? [literally: Who performs the repairs of things that are out of order?])

The main things to find out about a house are the following:

- ✔ **Eto dom v gorodye ili v prigorodye?** (eh-tuh dohm v goh-ruh-d'eh ee-lee f pree-guh-ruh-d'eh?; Is the house in the city or in the suburbs?)

- ✔ **Kakoj vid transporta tuda khodit?** (kuh-kohy veet trahn-spuhr-tuh too-dah khoh-deet?; Which public transportation runs there?)

✔ **Skol'ko v domye etazhyej?** (*skohl'*-kuh v *doh*-mee eh-tuh-*zhehy?;* How many floors does the house have?)

✔ **Kakoye v domye otoplyeniye?** (kuh-*koh*-eh v *doh*-m'eh uh-tah-*pl'eh*-nee-eh?; How is the house heated?)

✔ **V domye yest' garazh?** (v *doh*-m'eh yest' guh-*rahsh?;* Is there a garage in the house?)

Sealing the deal

When you find a place to rent that strikes your fancy, you're ready to **podpisat' kontrakt** (puhd-pee-*saht'* kahn-*trahkt;* sign the lease). In your **kontrakt na aryendu zhil'ya** (kahn-*trahkt* nuh uh-r'ehn-doo zhihl'-ya; lease), look for the following key points:

✔ **oplata/plata** (ah-*plah*-tuh/*plah*-tuh; rent)

✔ **podpis'** (*poht*-pees'; signature)

✔ **srok** (srohk; duration of the lease)

Settling Into Your New Digs

Congratulations on moving into your new home! In the following sections, you discover how to talk about your home and the things you have there.

Knowing the names of different rooms

Russians don't usually have as many rooms as Americans do. And the rooms they have are often reversible: a **divan-krovat'** (dee-*vahn* krah-*vaht';* sofa bed) can turn a cozy **gostinnaya** (gahs-*tee*-nuh-yuh; living room) into a **spal'nya** (*spahl'*-n'uh; bedroom). In the morning, the same room can magically turn into a **stolovaya** (stah-*loh*-vuh-yuh; dining room) when the hosts bring in their **skladnoj stol** (skluhd-*nohy* stohl; folding table)!

Here are some names for rooms to navigate you through a Russian apartment:

- **dyetskaya** (*d'eht*-skuh-yuh; children's room)
- **kabinyet** (kuh-bee-*n'eht*; study)
- **koridor** (kuh-ree-*dohr*; corridor)
- **kukhnya** (*kookh*-n'uh; kitchen)
- **prikhozhaya** (pree-*khoh*-zhuh-yuh; hall)

The English word *bathroom* corresponds to two different notions in Russian: **vannaya** (*vahn*-nuh-yuh) and **tualyet** (too-uh-*l'eht*). **Vannaya** is the place where the **vanna** (*vahn*-nuh; bathtub), **dush** (doosh; shower), and **rakovina** (*rah*-kuh-vee-nuh; sink) are. The **tualyet** is usually a separate room next to the **vannaya**.

One of the more important phrases in any language is this one: **Gdye tualyet?** (gd'eh too-uh-*l'eht?;* Where is the bathroom?)

Most Russian room names, such as **gostinnaya** and **stolovaya,** don't decline like nouns. Instead, they decline like feminine adjectives. The explanation to this mystery is easy: **Stolovaya** is what remained in modern Russian of **stolovaya komnata** (dining room), where the word **stolovaya** was, in fact, an adjective, describing the feminine noun **komnata** (room). (For more info on adjective declension, see Chapter 2.)

Buying furniture

The easiest place to find **myebyel'** (*m'eh*-beel'; furniture) is a **myebyel'nij magazin** (*m'eh*-beel'-nihy muh-guh-zeen; furniture store). Here are some Russian words for various pieces of furniture:

- **divan** (dee-*vahn;* sofa)
- **dukhovka** (doo-*khohf*-kuh; oven)
- **kholodil'nik** (khuh-lah-*deel'*-neek; refrigerator)

- ✔ **knizhnaya polka** (*kneezh*-nuh-yuh *pohl*-kuh; bookshelf)

- ✔ **kovyor** (kah-*vyor;* carpet/rug)

- ✔ **krovat'** (krah-*vaht';* bed)

- ✔ **kryeslo** (*kr'ehs*-luh; armchair)

- ✔ **kukhonnyj stol** (*koo*-khuh-nihy stohl; kitchen table)

- ✔ **lampa** (*lahm*-puh; lamp)

- ✔ **magnitofon** (muhg-nee-tah-*fohn;* stereo)

- ✔ **mikrovolnovka** (meek-ruh-vahl-*nohf*-kuh; microwave)

- ✔ **pis'myennyj stol** (pees'-mee-nihy stohl; desk/writing table)

- ✔ **plita** (plee-tah; stove)

- ✔ **posudomoyechnaya mashina** (pah-*soo*-dah-*moh*-eech-nuh-yuh muh-*shih*-nuh; dishwasher)

- ✔ **shkaf** (shkahf; cupboard/closet/wardrobe)

- ✔ **stiral'naya mashina** (stee-*rahl'*-nuh-yuh muh-*shih*-nuh; washing machine)

- ✔ **stol** (stohl; table)

- ✔ **stul** (stool; chair)

- ✔ **sushilka** (soo-*shihl*-kuh; dryer)

- ✔ **zhurnal'nyj stolik** (zhoor-*nahl'*-nihy *stoh*-leek; coffee table)

- ✔ **zyerkalo** (*z'ehr*-kuh-luh; mirror)

Booking the Hotel That's Right for You

Russian today has two words for the English *hotel:*

- ✔ **gostinitsa** (gahs-*tee*-nee-tsuh; hotel [*literally:* a place for the guests])

- ✔ **otel'** (ah-*tehl';* hotel)

Although from a linguistic point of view both words are interchangeable, they're charged with slightly different meanings. Nobody in Russia uses the word **otel** (hotel) in reference to a little old shabby hotel. In this situation, the word **gostinitsa** (hotel) is more appropriate. On the other hand, when speaking about luxurious four- or five-star hotels, Russians use both words interchangeably.

Making a reservation

To make a reservation, you want to say:

> **Ya khotyel/khotyela by zabronirovat' nomyer**
> (ya khah-*t'ehl*/khah-*t'eh*-luh bih zuh-brah-*nee*-ruh-vuht' *noh*-meer; I would like to make a reservation for a room).

Use **khotyel** if you're a man and **khotyela** if you're a woman.

When they talk about hotel rooms, Russians use the word **nomyer,** which also means "number." In a way it makes sense because each hotel room has a number!

After you state that you want to make a reservation, the person you're talking to will probably ask **Na kakoye chislo?** (nuh kuh-*koh*-ee chees-*loh?*; For what date?)

To answer, use this formula: **Na** (nah; for) + the ordinal numeral indicating date in neuter + the name of the month in genitive case. For example, if you're planning to arrive on September 15, you say: **Na pyatnadtsatoye syentyabrya** (nuh peet-*naht*-tsuh-tuh-eh seen-teeb-*r'ah;* For September 15).

You may also be asked from what date to what date you want to stay in the hotel: **S kakogo po kakoye**

chislo? (s kuh-*koh*-vuh puh kuh-*koh*-eh chees-*loh?*; From what date to what date?)

To answer this question, use **s** (s; from) + the genitive case of the ordinal number indicating the date + the genitive case of the word indicating the month + **po** (poh; until) + the ordinal numeral indicating the date in neuter gender (and nominative case) + name of the month in the genitive case. If, for example, you're planning to stay in the hotel from June 21 to June 25, you say **S dvadtsat' pyervogo iyunya po dvadtsat' pyatoye iyunya** (s *dvaht*-tsuht' *p'ehr*-vuh-vuh ee-*yoo*-n'uh p'ah *dvaht*-tsuht' *p'ah*-tuh-eh ee-*yoo*-n'uh; from June 21 to June 25).

You also can simply state how many nights you're going to stay in the hotel. If you're checking in on June 21 at 3 p.m. and leaving on June 25 at 11 a.m., you'll be staying in the hotel **chyetyrye nochi** (chee-*tih*-r'eh *noh*-chee; four nights).

Here are some other important phrases you may need to understand:

- ✔ **Vy khotitye odnomyestnyj nomyer ili dvukhmyestnyj nomyer?** (vih khah-*tee*-tee uhd-nah-*m'ehst*-nihy ee-lee dvookh-*m'ehst*-nihy *noh*-meer?; Do you want a single or double accommodation?)

- ✔ **V nomyere yest' vannaya, dush, i tualyet?** (v *noh*-mee-r'eh yest' *vah*-nuh-yuh, doosh, ee too-uh-*lyet?*; Is there a bathtub, shower, and toilet in the room?)

- ✔ **Skol'ko stoit nomyer?** (*skohl'*-kuh *stoh*-eet *noh*-m'ehr?; How much is the room?)

- ✔ **Skol'ko stoyat nomyera?** (*skohl'*-kuh stoh-yuht nuh-mee-*rah?*; How much are the rooms?)

- ✔ **Eto vklyuchayet zavtrak?** (*eh*-tuh fklyoo-*chah*-eht *zahf*-truhk?; Does it include breakfast?)

Checking In and Out

Congratulations! You made it to your hotel. To make
your check-in process as smooth as possible, in the
following sections, we tell you what to say when
checking in, how to find your room and what to
expect when you get there, and how to find what
you're looking for in the hotel. And then we tell you
how to check out.

Enduring the registration process

Look for a sign with the word **ryegistratsiya**
(ree-gee-*strah*-tsih-ye; check-in). That's where
you report your arrival. Simply say **U
myenya zabronirovan nomyer** (oo mee-*nya*
zuh-brah-*nee*-ruh-vuhn *noh*-meer; I have a
room reserved).

Expect to be asked **Kak vasha familiya?** (kahk *vah*-
shuh fuh-*mee*-lee-ye?; What is your last name?) Keep
your passport ready — you need it for registration.
To ask for your passport, the **dezhurnij administrator**
(dee-*zhoor*-nihy ahd-mee-neest-*rah*-tuhr; receptionist)
says: **Vash pasport** (vahsh *pahs*-puhrt; Your passport).

The next step in registration is filling out the
ryegistratsionnaya kartochka (ree-gee-struh-tsih-
oh-nuh-ye *kahr*-tuhch-kuh; registration form). You
hear **Zapolnitye, pozhalujsta, ryegistratsionnuyu
kartochku.** (zuh-*pohl*-nee-tee, pah-*zhahl*-stuh, ree-
gee-struh-tsih-*ohn*-noo-yu *kahr*-tuhch-koo; Fill out the
registration form, please.) In most cases, this form
requires you to provide the following information:

- ✔ **Imya** (*ee*-m'uh; first name)
- ✔ **Familiya** (fuh-*mee*-lee-yuh; last name)
- ✔ **Adryes** (*ahd*-rees; address)

✔ **Domashnij/rabochij tyelefon** (dah-*mahsh*-neey/ ruh-*boh*-cheey tee-lee-*fohn;* home/work phone number)

✔ **Srok pryebyvanya v gostinitsye s . . . po . . .** (srohk pree-bih-*vah*-nee-yuh v gahs-*tee*-nee-tseh s . . . pah . . . ; period of stay in the hotel from . . . to . . .)

✔ **Nomyer pasporta** (*noh*-meer *pahs*-puhr-tuh; passport number)

After you fill out all the forms and give the receptionist your passport, you receive the all-important **klyuch ot komnaty** (klyuch aht *kohm*-nuh-tih; key to your room) and your **kartochka gostya** (*kahr*-tuhch-kuh *gohs*-t'uh; hotel guest card) or **visitka** (vee-*zeet*-kuh; hotel guest card).

Don't assume that your room number is related to the floor number. For example, if the **nomyer komnaty** (*noh*-meer *kohm*-nuh-tih; room number) is 235, it doesn't mean that the room is on the second floor; it can actually be on any floor of the hotel. Before you leave **risepshn** (ree-*sehp*-shn; check-in), ask: **Na kakom etazhye moy nomyer?** (nuh kuh-*kohm* eh-tuh-*zheh* mohy *noh*-meer; On what floor is my room?)

Never leave the hotel without your **kartochka gostya** or **visitka** if you want to be let into the hotel. In most cases, you need to present the **visitka** to the security officer that most Russian hotels are staffed with today.

Taking a tour of your room

What can you expect to find in your hotel room? Most likely, you will see the following:

✔ **budil'nik** (boo-*deel'*-neek; alarm clock)

✔ **dvukhspal'naya krovat'** (dvookh-*spahl'*-nuh-yuh krah-*vaht';* double bed)

- ✔ **odnospal'nya krovat'**(uhd-nah-*spahl'*-nuh-yuh krah-*vaht';* twin bed)

- ✔ **pis'myonnyj stol I stul** (*pees*-mee-nihy stohl ee stool; desk and a chair)

- ✔ **shkaf** (shkahf; wardrobe)

- ✔ **torshyer** (tahr-*shehr;* standing lamp)

- ✔ **tumbochki** (*toom*-buhch-kee; nightstands)

- ✔ **tyelyefon** (tee-lee-*fohn;* telephone)

- ✔ **tyelyefonnyj spravochnik** (tee-lee-*foh*-nihy *sprah*-vuhch-neek; phone book containing hotel numbers)

- ✔ **tyelyevizor** (tee-lee-*vee*-zuhr; TV set)

- ✔ **vyeshalki** (*v'eh*-shuhl-kee; hangers)

If you have a bathroom in your room, you may find the following necessities:

- ✔ **dush** (doosh; shower)

- ✔ **lichnoye polotyentsye** (*leech*-nuh-eh puh-lah-*tyen*-tseh; towel)

- ✔ **unitaz** (oo-nee-*tahs;* toilet)

- ✔ **vannaya** (*vah*-nuh-yuh; bathtub)

- ✔ **vannoye polotyentsye** (*vah*-nuh-eh puh-lah-*t'ehn*-tseh; bath towel)

Familiarizing yourself with the facilities

To idle away time in the hotel, you may want to explore. Here's what you may find:

- ✔ **bahr** (bahr; bar)

- ✔ **byuro obsluzhivaniya** (byu-*roh* ahp-*sloo*-zhih-vuh-nee-yuh; customer service)

- ✔ **gardyerob** (guhr-dee-*rohp;* cloak room)

✔ **kamyera khranyeniya** (*kah*-mee-ruh khruh-*nye*-nee-yuh; storeroom)

✔ **pochta** (*pohch*-tuh; post office)

✔ **ryestoran** (rees-tah-*rahn*; restaurant)

✔ **suvyenirnyj kiosk** (soo-vee-*neer*-nihy kee-*ohsk*; souvenir kiosk)

To inquire where a certain service is, go to the **byuro obsluzhivaniya** and say **Skazhitye, pozhalujsta, gdye kamyera khranyeniya/pochta?** (skuh-*zhih*-tee pah-*zhah*-luh-stuh gdye *kah*-mee-ruh khruh-*nye*-nee-ee/*pohch*-tuh?; Could you tell me where the storeroom/post office is?)

Meeting the staff

People who work in the earlier-mentioned facilities and other hotel services you want to know include the following:

✔ **administrator** (uhd-mee-nee-*strah*-tuhr; manager, person working at the front desk, or concierge)

✔ **gardyerobsh'ik/gardyerobsh'tsa** (guhr-dee-*rohp*-sh'eek/guhr-dee-*rohp*-sh'ee-tsuh; a man/woman working in the cloak room)

✔ **gornichnaya** (*gohr*-neech-nuh-yuh; maid)

✔ **nosil'sh'ik** (nah-*seel'*-sh'eek; porter)

✔ **shvyejtsar** (shvehy-*tsahr;* doorman)

Reporting a broken item

A very common problem is when something in your room isn't working. The key refuses to open the door, the phone is silent when you pick it up, or the shower pours only cold water on you. You need to speak to a **rabotnik** (ruh-*boht*-neek; employee) in **byuro obsluzhivaniya** (byu-*roh* ahp-*sloo*-zhih-vuh-nee-ye; customer service) to get help for these problems.

To report the problem, use the phrase **U myenya v komnatye nye rabotayet . . .** (oo mee-*n'ah* f *kohm*-nuh-tee noo ruh *boh* tuh-cet, The . . . in my room is not working) + the item that's not working. If your telephone is broken, for instance, you say **U myenya v komnatye nye rabotayet tyelyefon** (oo mee-*n'ah* f *kohm*-nuh-t'eh nee ruh-*boh*-tuh-eet tee-lee-*fohn;* The telephone in my room is not working). You put the word for the broken item into the nominative case. (For more information on cases, see Chapter 2.)

Requesting missing items

The formula you need to know to report that something is missing is: **U myenya v nomyere nyet** (oo-mee-*n'ah* v *noh*-mee-r'eh nyet; In my room I don't have a) + the word denoting a missing thing, in the genitive case. (For more information on forming the genitive case, see Chapter 2.)

Imagine that you've just taken a shower and are now reaching for the **vannoye polotyentsye** (*vah*-nuh-ee puh-lah-*tyen*-tseh; bath towel) only to discover you don't have one! Shivering from cold and dripping water from your freshly showered body, you rush to the phone to call customer service. You say: **U myenya v nomyerye nyet vannogo polotyentsa** (oo mee-*nya* v *noh*-mee-ree nyet *vah*-nuh-vuh puh-lah-*tyen*-tsuh; I don't have a bath towel in my room). Other things that you may request include

- **odyeyalo** (ah-dee-*ya*-luh; blanket)
- **podushka** (pah-*doosh*-kuh; pillow)
- **tualyetnaya bumaga** (too-uh-*lyet*-nuh-ye boo-*mah*-guh; toilet paper)
- **vyeshalka** (*v'eh*-shuhl-kuh; hanger)

Asking to change rooms

To be honest, changing rooms isn't the easiest thing to do in a Russian hotel, but as they say in Russian: **Popytka nye pytka!** (pah-*piht*-kuh nee *piht*-kuh; It doesn't hurt to try! [*literally:* An attempt is not a torture!]) You should call customer service and say **Ya khotyel/khotyela by pomyenyat' nomyer** (ya khah-*tyel*/khah-*tye*-luh bih puh-mee-*nyat'* *noh*-meer; I would like to change my room). You say **khotyel** if you're a man and **khotyela** if you're a woman. And you need to give some convincing reasons for wanting to do so, such as:

- ✔ **V komnatye ochyen' shumno** (f *kohm*-nuh-t'eh *oh*-cheen' *shoom*-nuh; It is very noisy in my room).

- ✔ **V komnatye ochyen' kholodno/zharko** (f *kohm*-nuh-tee *oh*-cheen' *khoh*-luhd-nuh/*zhahr*-kuh; It is very cold/hot in my room).

- ✔ **V komnatye nyet svyeta** (f *kohm*-nuh-t'eh n'eht *sv'eh*-tuh; There is no light in my room).

Checking out and paying your bill

Your stay has come to an end, and now you have to pay. Or as Russians like to say: **Nastupil chas rasplaty** (nuh-stoo-*peel* chahs ruhs-*plah*-tih; It's time to pay [*literally:* The hour of reckoning has arrived]). Here are some phrases you'll need:

- ✔ **Ya khochu zaplatit'.** (ya khah-*choo* zuh-pluh-*teet';* I want to pay for my stay.)

- ✔ **Ya vypisyvayus'.** (ya vih-*pee*-sih-vuh-yoos'; I am checking out.)

- ✔ **Vy prinimayetye kryeditnyye kartochki?** (vih pree-nee-*mah*-ee-t'eh kree-*deet*-nih-ee *kahr*-tuhch-kee; Do you accept credit cards?)

✔ **Kakiye kryeditnyye kartochnki vy prini-mayetye?** (kuh-*kee*-ee kree-*deet*-nih-eh *kahr*-tuhch-kee vih pree-nee-*mah*-ee-tee; What credit cards do you take?)

As in most hotels throughout the world, the **rasschyotnyj chas** (ruhs-*chyot*-nihy chahs; check-out time) is **poldyen'** (*pohl*-deen'; noon) or **dvyenadtsat' chasov dnya** (dvee-*naht*-tsuht' chuh-*sohf* dn'ah; 12 p.m.). So where do you put your luggage if your plane doesn't leave until midnight? Most hotels have a **kamyera khranyeniya** (*kah*-mee-ruh khruh-*nye*-nee-yuh; storeroom).

Chapter 11

Dealing with Emergencies

. . . .

In This Chapter

▶ Knowing how to ask for help

▶ Getting medical attention

▶ Dealing with the police

. . . .

*A*n emergency would be called something else if being fully prepared for it were possible. However, you can avoid some panic if you know how to explain yourself in various unpleasant situations.

Finding Help in Case of Accidents

Dealing with accidents and emergencies in your native language is enough of a headache; problems seem twice as bad when you have to speak a foreign language to resolve them. But if you know how to ask for help, chances are, you'll find somebody who makes resolving your problems much easier.

Asking for help

The first thing you need to know is how to ask for help.

> ✔ **Izvinitye, mnye nuzhna pomosh'!** (eez-vee-*nee*-teh mnye noozh-*nah* poh-muhsh'; Excuse me, I need help!)

> ✔ **Pomogitye mn'e, pozhalujsta?** (puh-mah-*gee*-teh mnye pah-*zhah*-luh-stuh; Will you please help me?)

Use one of the following phrases to explain what's wrong:

> ✔ **Ya syebya plokho chuvstvuyu.** (ya see-*bya* ploh-khuh *choos*-tvoo-yu; I am not feeling well. [Use if you have a headache or other mild symptoms.])

> ✔ **Mnye plokho.** (mnye *ploh*-khuh; I am not feeling well. [Use if you are very, very sick — for example, you have intense pain or nausea, or you feel as though you may faint.])

> ✔ **Pozvonitye v skoruyu pomosh'!** (puhz-vah-*nee*-teh v *skoh*-roo-yu *poh*-muhsh'; Call an ambulance!)

> ✔ **Pomogitye!** (puh-mah-*gee*-tee; Help!)

> ✔ **Pozovitye na pomosh'!** (puh-zah-*vee*-teh nuh *poh*-muhsh'; Call for help!)

> ✔ **Pozvonitye v militsiyu!** (puhz-vah-*nee*-teh v mee-*lee*-tsih-yu; Call the police!)

> ✔ **Dyerzhitye vora!** (deer-*zhih*-teh *voh*-ruh; Stop the thief!)

> ✔ **Pozhar!** (pah-*zhahr*; Fire!)

To get help, you can also say **Ya nye mogu . . .** (ya nee mah-goo; I can't . . .) + the infinitive of the verb describing what it is you can't do. For instance, try the verb **najti** (nuhy-*tee*; to find) or **otkryt'** (aht-*kriht'*; to open), and then follow with the item you can't find or open.

Calling the right number

In the United States, calling 911 is the answer to almost any emergency question, but it's not this way in Russia. There, you have three different numbers to call in cases of **pozhar** (pah-*zhahr*; fire), crime, or health problems. The numbers are easy, and any Russian knows them by heart:

- ✔ **01 — pozharnaya sluzhba** (pah-*zhahr*-nuh-yuh *sloozh*-buh; fire brigade)
- ✔ **02 — militsiya** (mee-*lee*-tsih-yuh; police)
- ✔ **03 — skoraya pomosh'** (*skoh*-ruh-yuh *poh*-muhsh'; ambulance [*literally:* urgent help])

Two other easy numbers to remember:

- ✔ **04 — avarijnaja gazovaja sluzhba** (ah-vah-*reey*-nah-yuh *gah*-zuh-vuh-yuh *sloozh*-buh; the place where you call if you suspect gas leakage [*literally:* emergency gas service])
- ✔ **09 — spravochnaya** (*sprah*-vuhch-nuh-yuh; directory assistance)

Reporting a problem

When reporting an accident or an emergency, a good verb to use is **proiskhodit'** (pruh-ees-khah-*deet'*; to happen). To talk about something that is happening or has happened, you need only the third-person-singular form in the present tense — **proiskhodit** (pruh-ees-*khoh*-deet; is happening) — and the past-tense forms:

- ✔ **proizoshyol** (pruh-ee-zah-*shohl;* has happened [masculine singular])
- ✔ **proizoshla** (pruh-ee-zah-*shlah;* has happened [feminine singular])
- ✔ **proizoshlo** (pruh-ee-zah-*shloh;* has happened [neuter singular])
- ✔ **proizoshli** (pruh-ee-zah-*shlee;* has happened [plural])

A common question you may be asked if you've witnessed an accident is **Chto proizoshlo?** (shtoh pruh-ee-zah-*shloh;* What happened?) You may also hear **Chto sluchilos'?** (shtoh sloo-*chee*-luhs'; What happened?) The two phrases are interchangeable.

Problems that you may have to report include

- ✔ **avariya** (uh-*vah*-ree-yuh; car accident)
- ✔ **infarkt** (een-*fahrkt;* heart attack)
- ✔ **nyeschastnyj sluchaj** (nee-*shahs*-nihy sloo-chuhy; accident)
- ✔ **ograblyeniye** (uhg-ruhb-*lye*-nee-eh; robbery)
- ✔ **otravlyeniye** (uht-ruhv-*lye*-nee-eh; poisoning)
- ✔ **pozhar** (pah-*zhahr;* fire)
- ✔ **ranyeniye** (ruh-*nye*-nee-eh; injury)

Requesting English-speaking help

In case you don't feel like practicing your Russian in the midst of an emergency, you may want to ask for English-speaking help:

- ✔ **Zdyes' yest' kto-nibud', kto govorit po-anglijski?** (zdyes' yest' *ktoh*- nee-boot', ktoh guh-vah-*reet* puh uhng-*leey*-skee?; Is there anybody here who speaks English?)
- ✔ **Mnye nuzhyen kto-nibud', kto govorit po-anglijski!** (mnye *noo*-zhihn *ktoh*-nee-boot', ktoh guh-vah-*reet* puh uhng-*leey*-skee!; I need somebody who speaks English!)

Receiving Medical Care

To make an appointment with a specific doctor at a big **poliklinika** (puh-lee-*klee*-nee-kuh; clinic), you need to go to the **ryegistratura** (ree-gees-truh-*too*-ruh; check-in desk) and say **Mnye nado zapisat'sya na priyom k . . .** (mnye *nah*-duh zuh-pee-*saht'*-suh nuh pree-*yom* k . . . ; I need to make an appointment with . .) + the type of doctor you want to see (in the dative case). (For more information on case endings, see Chapter 2.)

Knowing your own anatomy

When you go to a doctor, you want to know how to talk about your **tyelo** (tye-*luh;* body). The following list starts with the visible parts, going from the top down:

- ✔ **golova** (guh-lah-*vah;* head)
- ✔ **gorlo** (*gohr*-luh; throat)
- ✔ **grud'** (groot'; chest/breast)
- ✔ **kolyeno** (kah-*l'eh*-nuh; knee)
- ✔ **kozha** (koh-zhuh; skin)
- ✔ **lodyzhka** (lah-*dihsh*-kuh; ankle)
- ✔ **lokot'** (*loh*-kuht'; elbow)
- ✔ **noga** (nah-*gah;* leg/foot)
- ✔ **nogti** (*nohk*-tee; nails)
- ✔ **palyets** (*pah*-leets; finger)
- ✔ **plyecho** (plee-*choh;* shoulder)
- ✔ **polovyye organy** (puh-lah-*vih*-eh *ohr*-guh-nih; genitals)
- ✔ **ruka** (roo-*kah;* arm/hand)
- ✔ **shyeya** (*sheh*-yuh; neck)
- ✔ **spina** (spee-*nah;* back)
- ✔ **zapyast'ye** (zuh-*pyast'*-yeh; wrist)
- ✔ **zhivot** (zhih-*voht;* stomach)

Russians do not emphasize the distinction between the arm and the hand; for both body parts, it is common to use the word **ruka.** Similarly, for both leg and foot, you use the word **noga.** However, if you want to specify the exact part of your **ruka** or **noga**, you can use the word **kist'** (keest'; hand), ladon' (lah-*dohn'*; palm) and **stupn'a** (stoop-*n'ah;* foot).

Parts of your head that you may seek treatment for include the following:

- **glaz** (glahs; eye)
- **litso** (lee-*tsoh;* face)
- **nos** (nohs; nose)
- **podborodok** (puhd-bah-*roh*-duhk; chin)
- **rot** (roht; mouth)
- **ukho** (*oo*-khuh; ear)
- **yazyk** (yee-*zihk;* tongue)
- **zub** (zoop; tooth)

The internal organs you may need to talk about include these body parts:

- **kost'** (kohst'; bone)
- **lyogkiye** (*lyokh*-kee-eh; lungs)
- **mozg** (mohsk; brain)
- **muskuly** (*moos*-koo-lih; muscles)
- **nyervy** (*n'er*-vih; nerves)
- **pochka** (*pohch*-kuh; kidney)
- **pyechyen'** (*pye*-chihn'; liver)
- **syerdtsye** (*syer*-tseh; heart)
- **zhyeludok** (zhih-*loo*-duhk; stomach)

Describing your symptoms to a doctor

The first question you hear from a doctor is usually **Chto u vas bolit?** (shtoh u vahs bah-*leet?;* What is hurting you?) or **Chto vas byespokoit?** (shtoh vahs bees-pah-*koh*-eet?; What brought you here? [*literally:* What is bothering you?])

The best way to start describing your symptoms if you're in pain is with the verb **bolyet** (bah-l'eht'; to hurt):

> **U myenya bolit . . .** (oo mee-*nya* bah-*leet* . . . ; . . . is hurting) + the name of the organ that hurts (in the nominative case).

You can also point to the place where it hurts and say

> **U myenya bolit zdyes'** (oo mee-*n'ah* bah-*leet* zdyes'; It hurts me here).

You may want to specify whether it hurts **vnutri** (vnoo-*tree;* inside) or **snaruzhi** (snah-*roo*-zhih; on the outside).

To describe specific, less-painful symptoms, you say **U myenya . . .** (oo mee-*nya;* I have . . .) + one of the phrases from the following list:

- ✔ **bol'** (bohl'; pain)
- ✔ **bolit golova** (bah-*leet* guh-lah-*vah;* headache)
- ✔ **bolit gorlo** (bah-*leet* gohr-luh; sore throat)
- ✔ **bolit ukho** (bah-*leet* oo-khuh; earache)
- ✔ **bolit zhivot** (bah-*leet* zhih-*voht;* stomach ache)
- ✔ **kashyel'** (*kah*-shihl'; cough)
- ✔ **nasmork** (*nahs*-muhrk; runny nose)
- ✔ **ozhog** (ah-*zhohk*; burn)
- ✔ **ponos** (pah-*nohs;* diarrhea)
- ✔ **syp'** (sihp'; rash)
- ✔ **toshnota** (tuhsh-nah-*tah;* nausea)
- ✔ **tyempyeratura** (teem-pee-ruh-*too*-ruh; fever)
- ✔ **zapor** (zuh-*pohr;* constipation)

In Russia, temperature is measured in Celsius. Normal body temperature is 36.6°C. Anything above is a **vysokaya tyempyer-atura** (vih-*soh*-kuh-ye teem-pee-ruh-*too*-ruh; high fever).

Announcing allergies or special conditions

To tell your doctor about any allergies, you can say **U myenya allyergiya na . . .** (oo mee-*nya* uh-leer-*gee*-ye nuh . . . ; I am allergic to . . .) + the word naming the cause of the allergy (in the accusative case). Common causes of allergies include

- **koshki** (*kohsh*-kee; cats)
- **mollyuski** (mah-*l'oos*-kee; shellfish)
- **moloko** (muh-lah-*koh;* milk)
- **obyezbolivayush'yeye** (uh-beez-*boh*-lee-vuh-yoo-sh'ee-ee; painkillers)
- **oryekhi** (ah-*rye*-khee; nuts)
- **plyesyen'** (*plye*-seen'; mold)
- **pyenitsillin** (pee-nee-tsih-*leen;* penicillin)
- **pyl'tsa** (pihl'-*tsah;* pollen)
- **ryba** (*rih*-buh; fish)
- **sobaki** (sah-*bah*-kee; dogs)
- **ukus pchyely** (oo-*koos* pchee-*lih;* bee stings)
- **yajtsa** (*yahy*-tsuh; eggs)

If you're on some kind of medication, tell your doctor **Ya prinimayu . . .** (ya pree-nee-*mah*-yoo . . . ; I am on . . . [*literally:* I take . . .]) + the name of the medication. Some other special conditions that you may need to announce to the doctor include

✔ **U myenya astma.** (oo mee-*n'ah ahst*-muh; I have asthma.)

✔ **Ya yepilycptiit.** (ya ee-~~pee~~-*'ehp*-~~teek~~; I have epilepsy.)

✔ **Ya diabyetik.** (ya dee-uh-*beh*-teek; I have diabetes.)

✔ **Ya byeryemyenna.** (ya bee-*r'eh*-mee-nuh; I am pregnant.)

Undergoing an examination and getting a diagnosis

During a medical exam, you may hear the following phrases:

✔ **Razdyen'tyes' do poyasa.** (ruhz-*dyen'*-tees' duh *poh*-ee-suh; Undress from your waist up.)

✔ **Razdyen'tyes' polnost'yu.** (ruhz-*dyen'*-tees' *pohl*-nuhst'-yoo; Take off all your clothes.)

✔ **Zakataytye rukav.** (zuh-kuh-*tahy*-teh roo-*kahf;* Please roll up your sleeve.)

✔ **Gluboko vdokhnitye.** (gloo-bah-*koh* vdahkh-*nee*-teh; Take a deep breath.)

✔ **Lozhityes'.** (lah-*zhih*-tees'; Please lie down.)

✔ **Otkrojtye rot.** (aht-*krohy*-teh roht; Open your mouth.)

✔ **Pokazhityte yazyk.** (puh-kuh-*zhih*-teh yee-*zihk;* Stick out your tongue.)

You also may have to undergo the following tests:

✔ **analiz krovi** (uh-*nah*-leez *kroh*-vee; blood test)

✔ **analiz mochi** (uh-*nah*-leez mah-*chee;* urine test)

✔ **ryentgyen** (reen-*gyen;* X-ray)

✔ **sonogramma** (suh-nah-*grah*-muh; sonogram)

✔ **ul'trazvuk** (ool'-truh-*zvook;* ultrasound)

✔ **elyektrokardiogramma** (ee-*l'ehkt*-ruh-kuhr-dee-ahg-*rah*-muh; electrocardiogram)

After all the turmoil of going through the **osmotr** (ahs-*mohtr;* medical examination), you're ready to hear your **diagnoz** (dee-*ahg*-nuhs; diagnosis). The doctor will probably phrase it this way: **U vas . . .** (oo vahs . . . ; you have . . .) + the diagnosis itself. For instance, you may hear that you have one of the following:

- ✔ **angina** (uhn-*gee*-nuh; sore throat)
- ✔ **bronkhit** (brahn-*kheet;* bronchitis)
- ✔ **gripp** (greep; flu)
- ✔ **infyektsiya** (een-*fyek*-tsih-yuh; infection)
- ✔ **migryen'** (mee-*gr'ehn';* migraine)
- ✔ **pnyevmoniya** (pneev-mah-*nee*-yuh; pneumonia)
- ✔ **prostuda** (prahs-*too*-duh; cold)
- ✔ **rastyazhyeniye svyazok** (ruhs-tee-*zheh*-nee-eh *sv'ah*-zuhk; sprain)
- ✔ **syennaya likhoradka** (*see*-nuh-yuh lee-khah-*raht*-kuh; hay fever)

Visiting a pharmacy

In most cases, a doctor will **propisat' lyekarstvo** (pruh-pee-*saht'* lee-*kahrst*-vuh; prescribe a medicine) for you. The Russian word for prescription is **ryet-syept** (ree-*tsehpt*).

The Russian word **ryetsyept** is an interpreter's false friend. To an English speaker, it sounds a lot like *receipt*. Watch out, though! The Russian for *receipt* is **chyek** (chehk). **Ryetsyept,** on the other hand, means "prescription" or "recipe."

To get your **lyekarstvo,** you need to go to the **aptyeka** (uhp-*tye*-kuh; pharmacy). To get your **lyekarstvo,** you hand your **ryetsyept** to the **aptyekar'** (uhp-*tye*-kuhr'; pharmacist). Alternately, you can say

- ✔ **Mnye nuzhyen . . .** (mn'eh *noo*-zhihn . . . ; I need . . .) + the masculine name of the medicine

✔ **Mnye nuzhna . . .** (mn'eh noozh-*nah* . . . ;
I need . . .) + the feminine name of the medicine

✔ **Mnye nuzhno . . .** (mn'eh noozh-*nuh* . . . ;
I need . . .) + the neuter name of the medicine

✔ **Mnye nuzhny . . .** (mn'eh noozh-*nih;* I need . . .)
+ the plural name of the medicines

Some common medicines include

✔ **aspirin** (uhs-pee-*reen;* aspirin)

✔ **bolyeutolyayush'yeye** (boh-lee-oo-tuh-*l'ah*-yu-
sh'ee-eh; pain reliever)

✔ **kapli ot kashlya** (*kahp*-lee uht *kahsh*-l'eh; cough
drops)

✔ **nyejtralizuyush'yeye kislotu sryedstvo** (neey-
truh-lee-*zoo*-yoo-sh'ih-yeh kees-lah-*too* sryets-
tvuh; antacid)

✔ **sirop ot kashlya** (see-*rohp* uht *kahsh*-lyuh;
cough syrup)

✔ **sryedstvo dlya snizhyeniya tyempyeratury**
(*sryets*-tvuh dlya snee-*zheh*-nee-uh teem-pee-
ruh-*too*-rih; fever reducer)

✔ **sryedstvo ot izzhyogi** (*sryets*-tvuh uht eez-*zhoh*-
gee; heartburn reliever)

Calling the Police When You're the Victim of a Crime

If you're the victim of crime, you need to know where
to turn to for help and what to say to the people help-
ing you.

To find the nearest police station, you can ask a
passerby **Gdye blizhajshyeye otdyelyeniye militsii?**
(gdye blee-*zhahy*-shih-ee uht-dee-*lye*-nee-ye mee-*lee*-
tsih-ee?; Where is the nearest police station?)

Here are some useful phrases you can use to describe different types of crime to the police:

- ✔ **Myenya ograbili.** (mee-*n'ah* ah-*grah*-bee-lee; I was robbed.)

- ✔ **Myenya obokrali.** (mee-*n'ah* uh-bah-*krah*-lee; I became a victim of a theft.)

- ✔ **Na myenya bylo sovyershyeno napadyeniye.** (nuh mee-*n'ah* *bih*-luh suh-veer-shih-*noh* nuh-puh-*d'eh*-nee-eh; I was attacked.)

- ✔ **Moyu kvartiru obvorovali.** (mah-*yoo* kvahr-*tee*-roo uhb-vuh-rah-*vah*-lee; My apartment was broken into.)

- ✔ **Ya stal zhyertvoj moshyennichyestva.** (ya stahl *zhehr*-tvohy muh-*sheh*-nee-cheest-vuh; I became a victim of a fraud [masculine].)

- ✔ **Ya stala zhyertvoj moschyennichyestva.** (ya *stah*-lah *zhehr*-tvuhy muh-*sheh*-nee-chihst-vuh; I became a victim of a fraud [feminine].)

- ✔ **Moyu mashinu obokrali.** (mah-*yu* muh-*shih*-noo uh-bahk-*rah*-lee; My car was broken into. [*literally:* My car was robbed.])

Chapter 12

Ten Favorite Russian Expressions

• •

*E*very culture has a way of taking familiar words and turning them into something else. Recognizing these expressions in speech and using them with ease can make you sound really Russian!

Oj!

To express surprise, dismay, admiration, gratitude, or even pain — pretty much any strong feeling — Russians say **Oj!** (ohy). Use **oj** when in English you would say "oops," "ouch," or "wow," or make a facial expression. You can confidently use **oj** in any of the following sentences:

- ✔ **Oj, kak krasivo!** (ohy kahk kruh-*see*-vuh; Wow, how beautiful!)
- ✔ **Oj, spasibo!** (ohy spuh-*see*-buh; Thank you so much!)
- ✔ **Oj, kto eto?** (ohy ktoh *eh*-tuh; Who in the world is this?)

Davaj

If you look up **davaj** (duh-*vahy*) in the dictionary, it means "give." Russians, however, use the word in all kinds of situations. It's a popular way to suggest doing something, as in **Davaj pojdyom v kino** (duh-*vahy* pahy-*d'ohm* v kee-*noh;* Let's go to the movies), and to answer "Sure, let's do it!" (**Davaj!**) Used by itself, **davai** means "Bye, take care."

Pryedstav'tye Syebye

Although the verb **pryedstav'tye** can mean "imagine," "picture," or even "introduce," **pryedstav'tye syebye** (preed-*stahf'*-te'h see-*b'eh*) means "Can you believe it?" or "Imagine that!" It's a good way to begin telling a story, or to open a conversation on a subject you feel strongly about.

Poslushajtye!

The literal translation of **Poslushajtye!** (pahs-*loo*-shuhy-te'h) is "Listen!" Although this sounds pushy and aggressive in English, in Russian, **poslushajtye** is a nice way to attract attention to your arguments. Here are some examples:

✔ **Poslushajtye, davajtye pojdyom na progulku!** (pahs-*loo*-shuhy-t'eh, duh-*vahy*-t'eh pahy-*d'ohm* nuh prah-*gool*-koo; You know what? Let's go for a walk! [*literally:* Listen, let's go for a walk!])

✔ **Poslushajtye, no eto zhe pryekrasnyj fil'm!** (pahs-*loo*-shuhy-t'eh, noh *eh*-tuh zheh preek-*rahs*-nihy feel'm; But it's a wonderful movie! [*literally:* Listen, but it's a wonderful movie!])

 A less formal variant of the same expression is **Poslushaj!** (pahs-*loo*-shuhy). You can use it with someone you're on familiar terms with.

Pir Goroj

You may be at a loss to describe the grand abundance of Russian dinner parties and holiday tables. This expression, then, is useful: **pir goroj** (peer gah-*rohy;* *literally:* feast with food piled up like a mountain).

Ya Tryebuyu Prodolzhyeniya Bankyeta

This phrase is a quote from one of the Russians' most beloved comedies, ***Ivan Vasil'yevich myenyayet profyessiyu*** (ee-*vahn* vah-*seel'*-ye-veech mee-*n'ah*-eht prah-*f'eh*-see-yoo; *Ivan Vasil'yevich Changes His Occupation*), and is sure to make any Russian smile. Say **Ya tryebuyu prodolzhyeniya bankyeta!** (ya *tr'eh*-boo-yu pruh-dahl-*zheh*-nee-uh buhn-*k'eh*-tuh; *literally:* I insist on the continuation of the banquet!) when a party or a trip is going well, when somebody is inviting you to come over again, or when you're suggesting to do some fun activity yet another time.

Slovo — Syeryebro, A Molchaniye — Zoloto

Russians love proverbs and use them a lot. **Slovo — syeryebro, a molchaniye — zoloto** (*sloh*-vuh see-reeb-*roh* uh mahl-*chah*-nee-eh *zoh*-luh-tuh; A word is silver, but silence is gold) can be loosely translated as "Speaking is nice, but silence is supreme." This phrase is nice to say after you make a mistake speaking Russian or when you, or somebody else, says something that would be better off left unsaid.

Odna Golova Khorosho, A Dvye — Luchshye

Odna golova khorosho, a dvye — luchshye (ahd-*nah* guh-lah-*vah* khuh-rah-*shoh* ah dv'eh *looch*-sheh; One head is good, but two heads are better) doesn't refer to science-fiction mutants. Rather, it's a manifestation of the international belief that two heads are better than one. You can say this phrase when you invite somebody to do something together or when you ask for, or offer, help or advice.

Drug Poznayotsya V Byedye

Drug poznayotsya v byedye (drook puhz-nah-*yot*-suh v bee-*d'eh;* A friend is tested by hardship) is the Russian equivalent of the saying, "A friend in need is a friend indeed."

Russians take friendship seriously. Their def-inition of a friend is not just a person you know (as in, "This is my new friend . . . what's your name again?"). Such a person would be called a **znakomyj** (znuh-*koh*-mihy; acquaintance). A **drug** (drook; friend), on the other hand, is someone who cares for you.

Staryj Drug Luchshye Novykh Dvukh

Staryj drug luchshye novykh dvukh (*stah*-rihy drook *looch*-sheh *noh*-vihkh dvookh; An old friend is better than two new ones) is another speculation on the theme of friendship. An old friend (and they aren't referring to age) is better because he or she has already been tested, possibly by hardships mentioned in the previous phrase. New friends, on the other hand, are dark horses; when a bad moment strikes, they may turn out to be just acquaintances.

Chapter 13

Ten Phrases That Make You Sound Russian

• •

Some phrases aren't really important in a conversation, but they make you sound Russian.

Tol'ko Poslye Vas!

Oh, dear Old World! Russians still believe in opening doors for each other and letting others go first. If you want to be especially polite, absolutely refuse to go through a door if somebody else is aiming for it. Instead of just walking through and getting it over with, stand by the door for 15 minutes repeating **Tol'ko poslye vas!** (*tohl'*-kuh *pohs*-lee vahs; Only after you!) while your counterpart stands by the other side of the door repeating the same phrase. It may be time consuming, but you'll be recognized as a well-bred individual.

Vy Syegodnya Pryekrasno Vyglyaditye!

Speaking of being old-fashioned: Russians, for some reason, don't believe that giving compliments is considered sexual harassment. So, if you start a conversation with a Russian woman by saying **Vy syegodnya pryekrasno vyglyaditye!** (vih see-*vohd*-n'uh pree-*krahs*-nuh *vihg*-lee-dee-t'eh; You look great today!), she may actually treat you nicer instead of reporting you to the authorities.

If someone says **Vy syegodnya pryekrasno vyglyadi-tye!** to you, remember that the appropriate response isn't **spasibo** (spuh-*see*-buh; thank you); you should say **Nu, chto vy!** (noo shton vih, Ah, what are you talking about!) You have to show your modesty and disagree.

Zakhoditye Na Chaj!

Making a Russian friend is very easy. When you meet someone (and if you like this person enough to want to be his or her friend), don't think too hard about finding a way to create a social connection. Just say **Zakhoditye na chaj!** (zuh-khah-*dee*-t'eh nuh chahy; Stop by for some tea!) The person won't think you're a freak or a serial killer; he or she will most likely take your offer at face value. Keep in mind, though, that unlike "Let's do lunch," Russians take **Zakhoditye na chaj** seriously and usually accept your offer. That being said, you should actually have some tea and cookies at home, because **Zakhoditye na chaj!** implies drinking tea and conversing, unlike the American version: "Would you like to stop by my place for a drink?"

Ugosh'ajtyes'!

When you invite a new friend over for tea and whip out your strategically prepared box of cookies, a nice thing to say is **Ugosh'ajtyes!** (oo-gah-*sh'ahy*-t'ehs'; Help yourself! [*literally:* Treat yourself!]) Besides being friendly and polite, this word is just long enough to scare off foreigners. Which is, of course, a good enough reason to learn it and stand out in the crowd.

Priyatnogo Appetita!

Unless you want to strike people as a gloomy, misan-thropic sociopath, don't start eating without wishing others **Priyatnogo appetita!** (pree-*yat*-nuh-vuh uh-pee-*tee*-tuh; *Bon appétit!*) Don't hesitate to say this phrase to people you don't know and are seeing for the first time in your life after your waiter sits them down at your table in an over-crowded restaurant.

Syadyem Na Dorozhku!

Before departing on a trip, surprise everybody by looking around thoughtfully and saying **Syadyem na dorozhku!** (*sya*-deem nuh dah-*rohsh*-koo; Let's sit down before hitting the road!) Essentially a supersti-tion, this tradition is actually useful; sitting down and staying silent for a minute before you head out the door gives you an opportunity to remember what's important. Maybe your packed lunch is still in the fridge, and your plane tickets with a sticker saying "Don't forget!" are still on your bedside table!

Sadis', V Nogakh Pravdy Nyet

Sitting down is a big deal for Russians. Which is, of course, understandable: With those vast lands, they must have had to walk a lot (especially before the invention of trains). That's why when you're sitting with somebody standing before you, or when some-body stops by and hangs out in the doorway, claiming to be leaving in a minute, you can say **Sadis', v nogakh pravdy nyet** (sah-*dees'*, v nah-*gahkh prahv*-dih n'eht; take the weight off your feet/it is as cheap sitting as standing).

Ni Pukha, Ni Pyera!

Although English has its own cute little "Break a leg" phrase, nobody really uses it anymore. Russians, on the other hand, never let anyone depart on a mission — whether a lady leaves to interview for a job or guy goes to ask a girl out — without saying **Ni pukha, ni pyera!** (nee *poo*-khuh nee pee-*rah;* Good luck! [*literally:* Have neither fluff nor plume!])

The appropriate response isn't **spasibo** (spuh-*see*-buh; thank you); you should say **K chyortu!** (k *chohr*-too; To the devil!)

Tseluyu

Russians sign their letters, e-mails, and cell phone text messages with **Tseluyu** (tsih-*loo*-yu; kisses [*literally:* (I am) kissing (you)]). You can also say **Tseluyu** at the end of a phone conversation. We don't recommend saying it in person, though: If you're face to face with someone, you may as well kiss the person instead of talking about it!

S Lyogkim Parom!

Here's a weird one: When Russians see someone who just came out of a shower, a sauna, or any place where you can, supposedly, clean yourself, they say **S lyogkim parom!** (s *lyokh*-keem pah-ruhm; *literally:* Congratulations on a light steam!)

You can use **S lyogkim parom!** humorously: Say it to someone who got caught in the rain or someone who spilled a drink. Yes, it sounds mean, but Russians have a dark sense of humor.

Index

• T •

FOR DUMMIES®

The easy way to get more done and have more fun